Hearts
And
Flowers
Mini
Coloring
Book

By Artist
Dwyanna Stoltzfus

Join the Fun!!
Share your colored pages!!

You are invited to color the pages

From this and all publications by

Dwyanna Stoltzfus. Then scan and post

Your colored creations in

"Coloring with Dwyanna"

Adult Coloring Group

On facebook

https://www.facebook.com/groups/1519357628356169/

Join Coloring with Dwyanna Adult Coloring Group,

And have fun sharing your colored pages

And meeting new coloring friends.

Members of the group will also have access

To free coloring pages.

You are welcome to share your colored pages on

Any social network, make sure to mention the title of

The book and the author/artist name.

Uncolored images may not be shared.

You are invited to view Dwyanna's art on

Society 6 at

https://society6.com/dwyanna

where additional items to color is available. Dwyanna

now has her beautiful designs on t-shirts, tank tops,

hoodies, tote bags, wall tapestries, pillows and

canvases.

Follow Dwyanna's art on facebook at

Oodles of Doodles Designs-

Adult Coloring Books by Dwyanna Stoltzfus

https://www.facebook.com/Oodles-of-Doodles-Designs-Adult-Coloring-

Books-by-Dwyanna-Stoltzfus-743502922387046/

Acknowledgments

Thank You to my family for all your support of my

Art and this project. I could not have done it without you!!

Thank You God for the gift and love

Of art and drawing!!

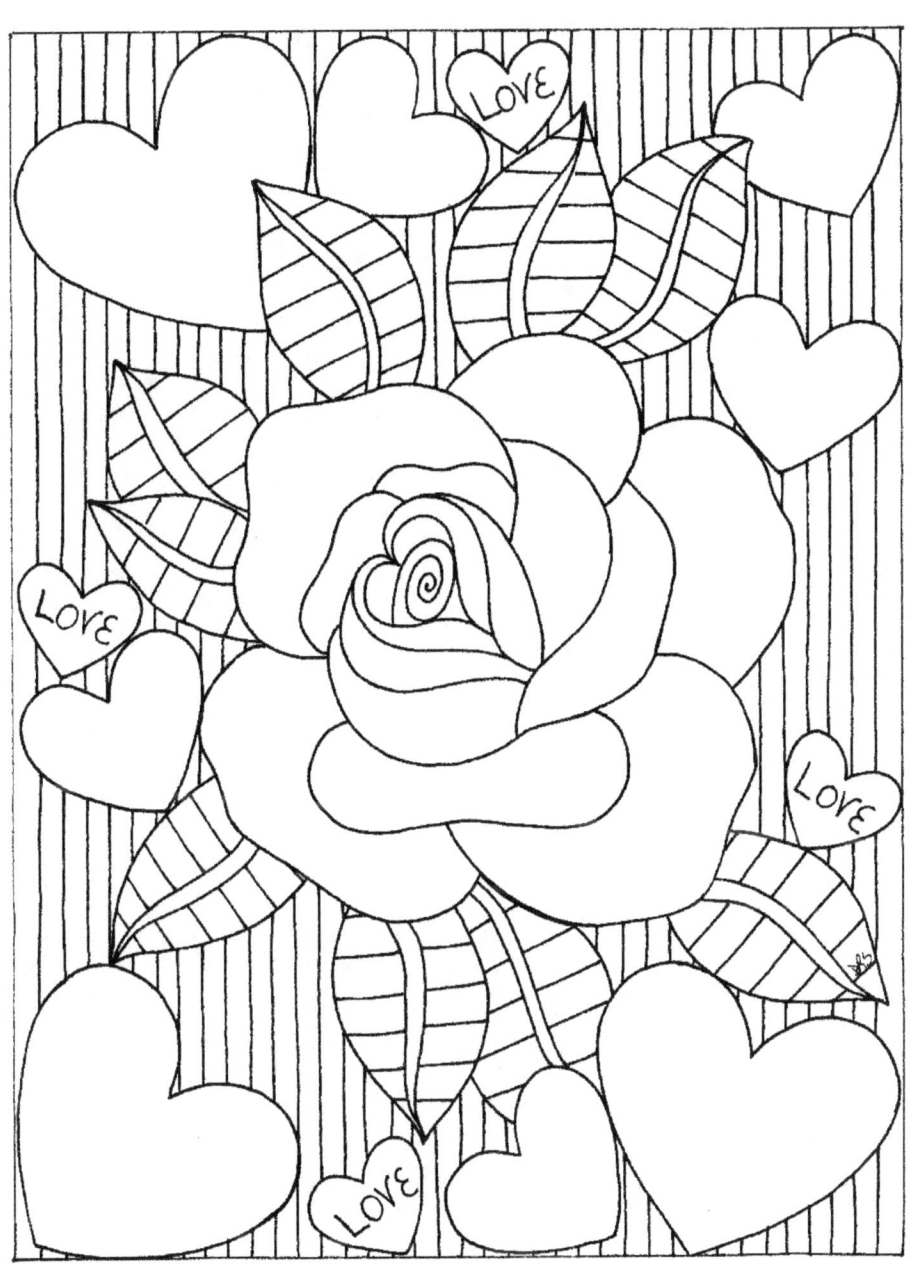

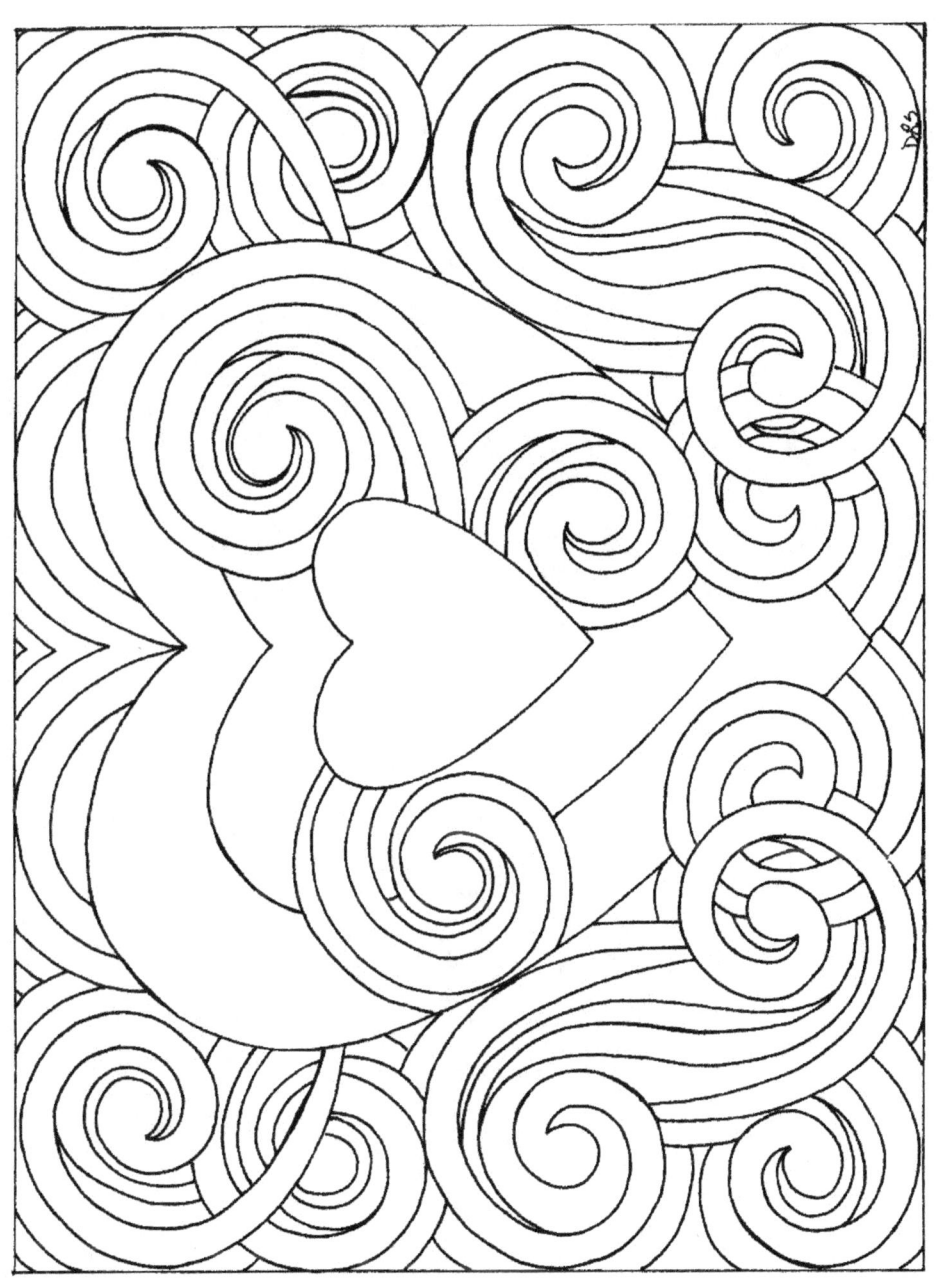

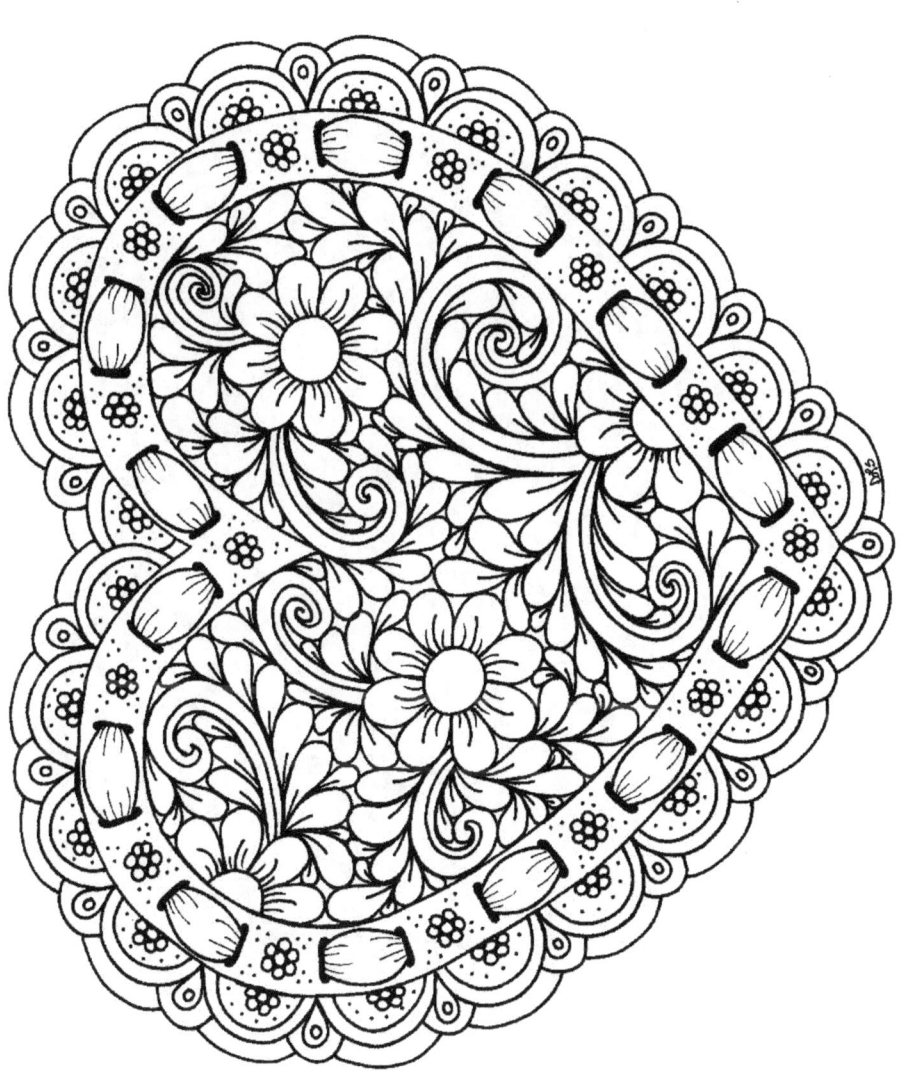

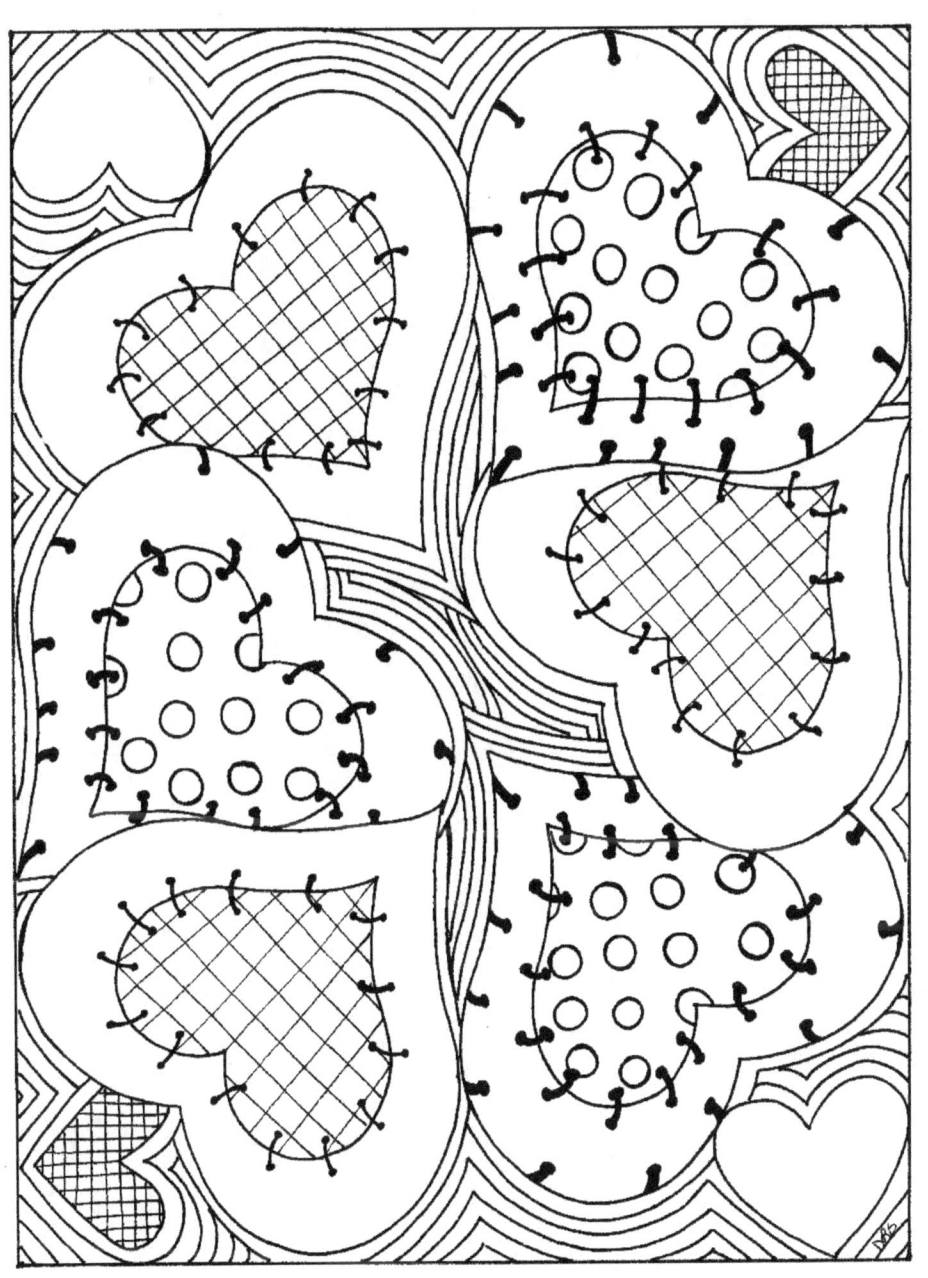

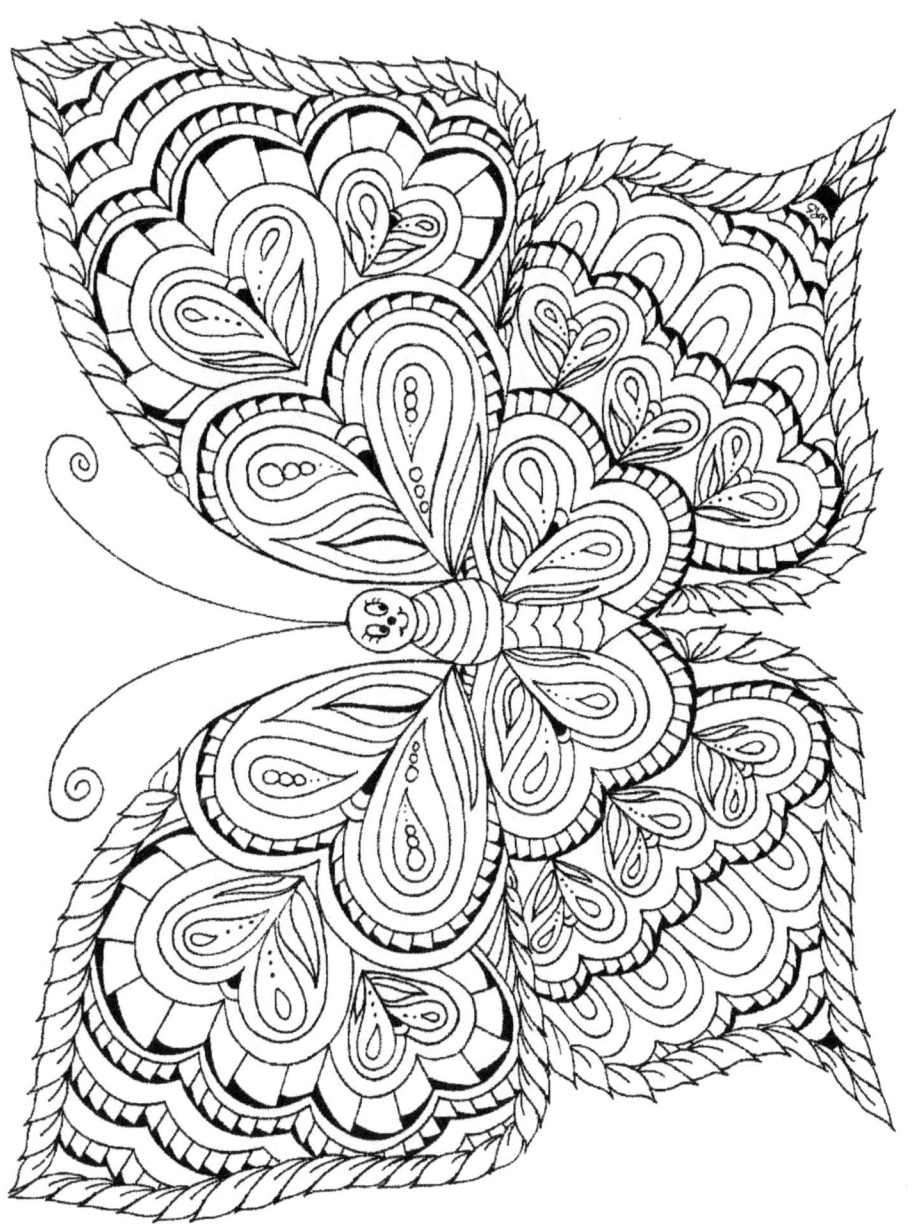

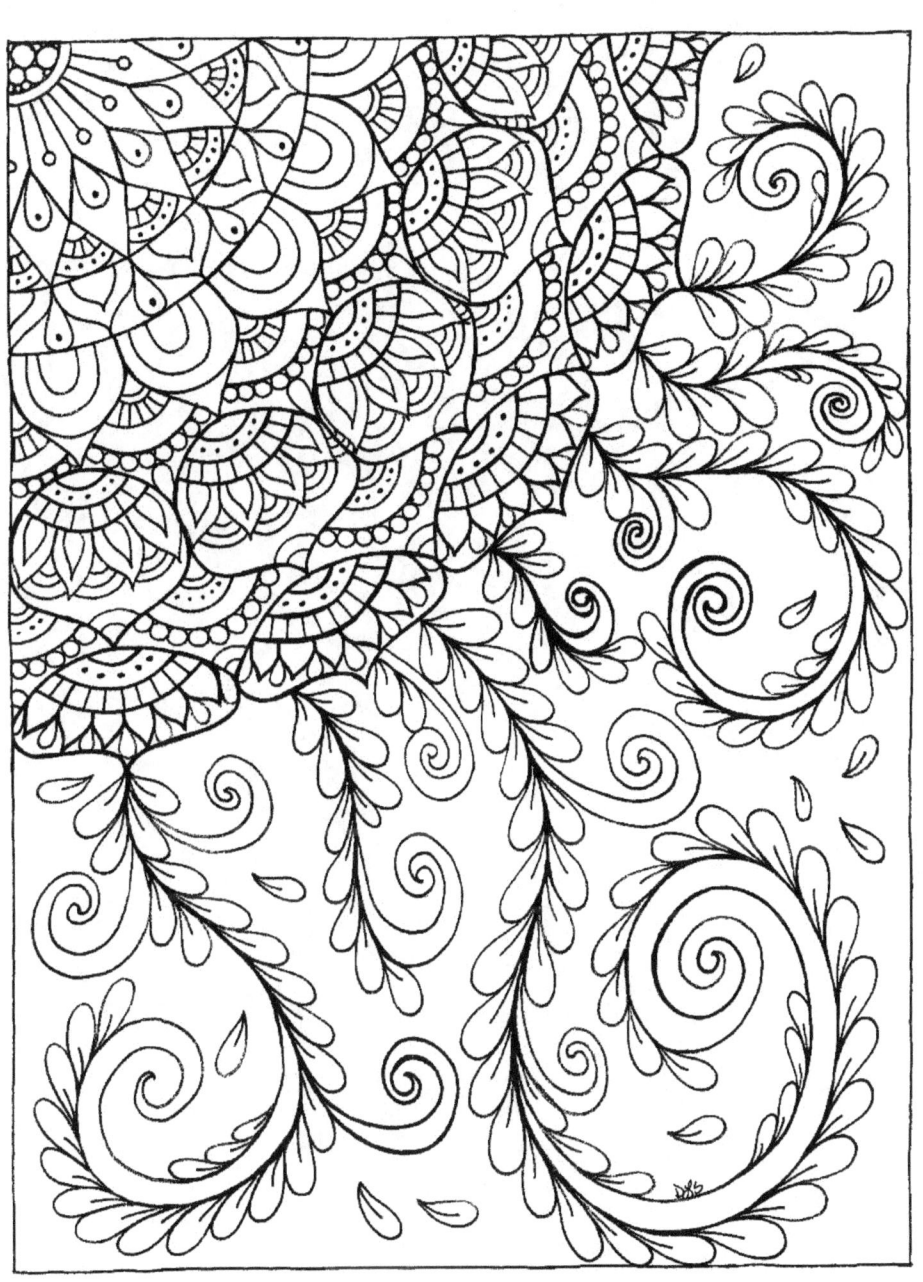

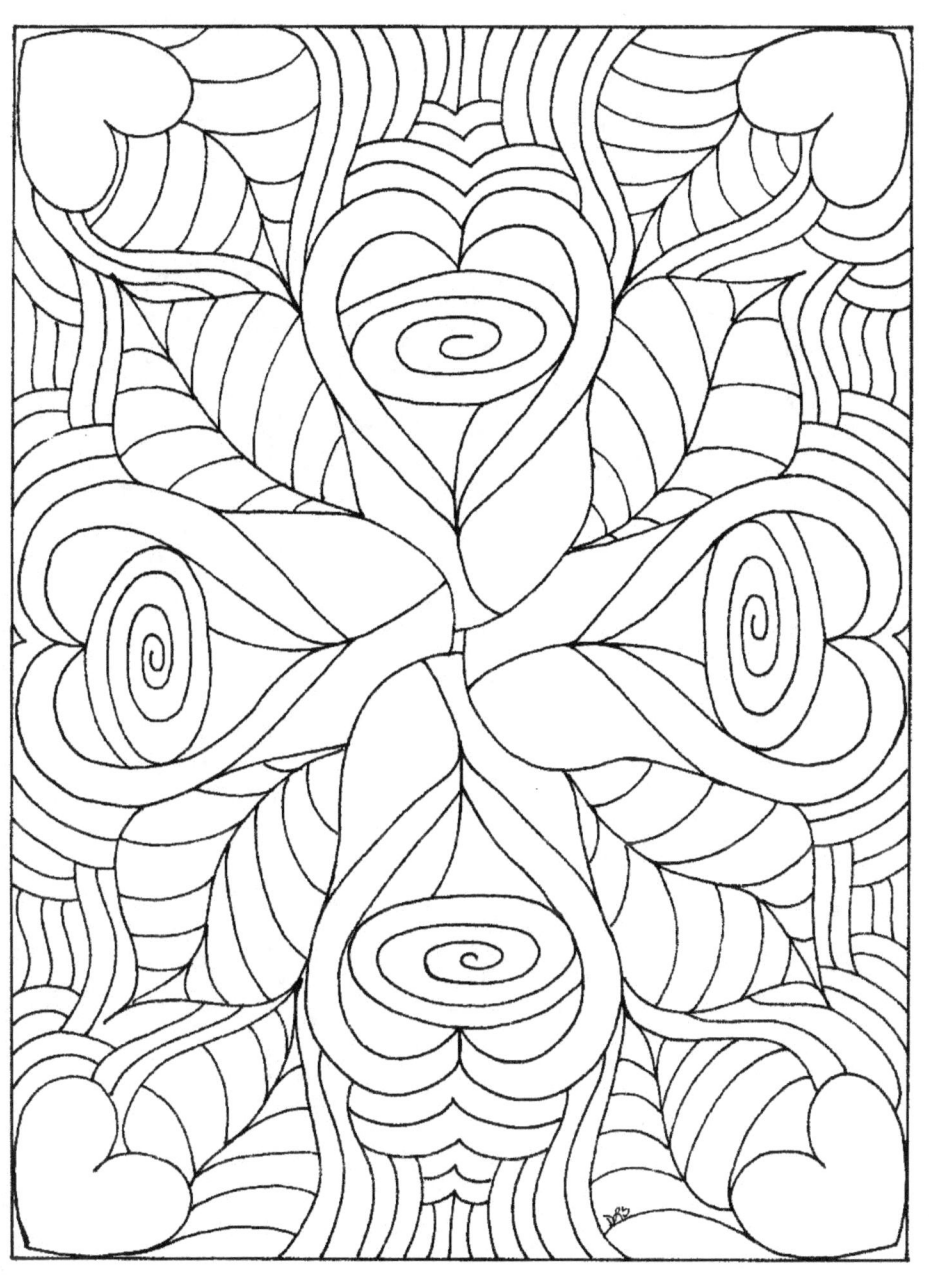

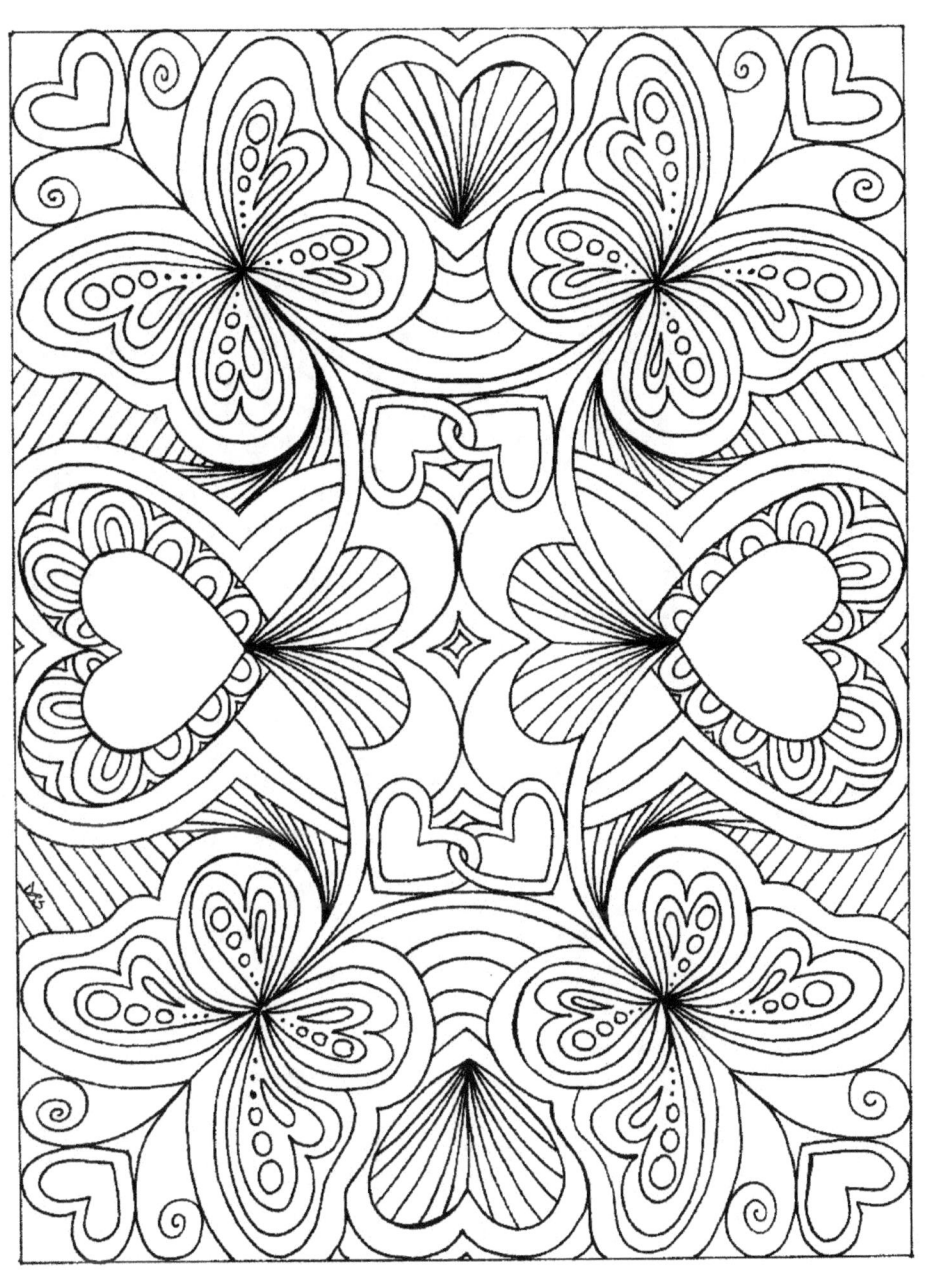

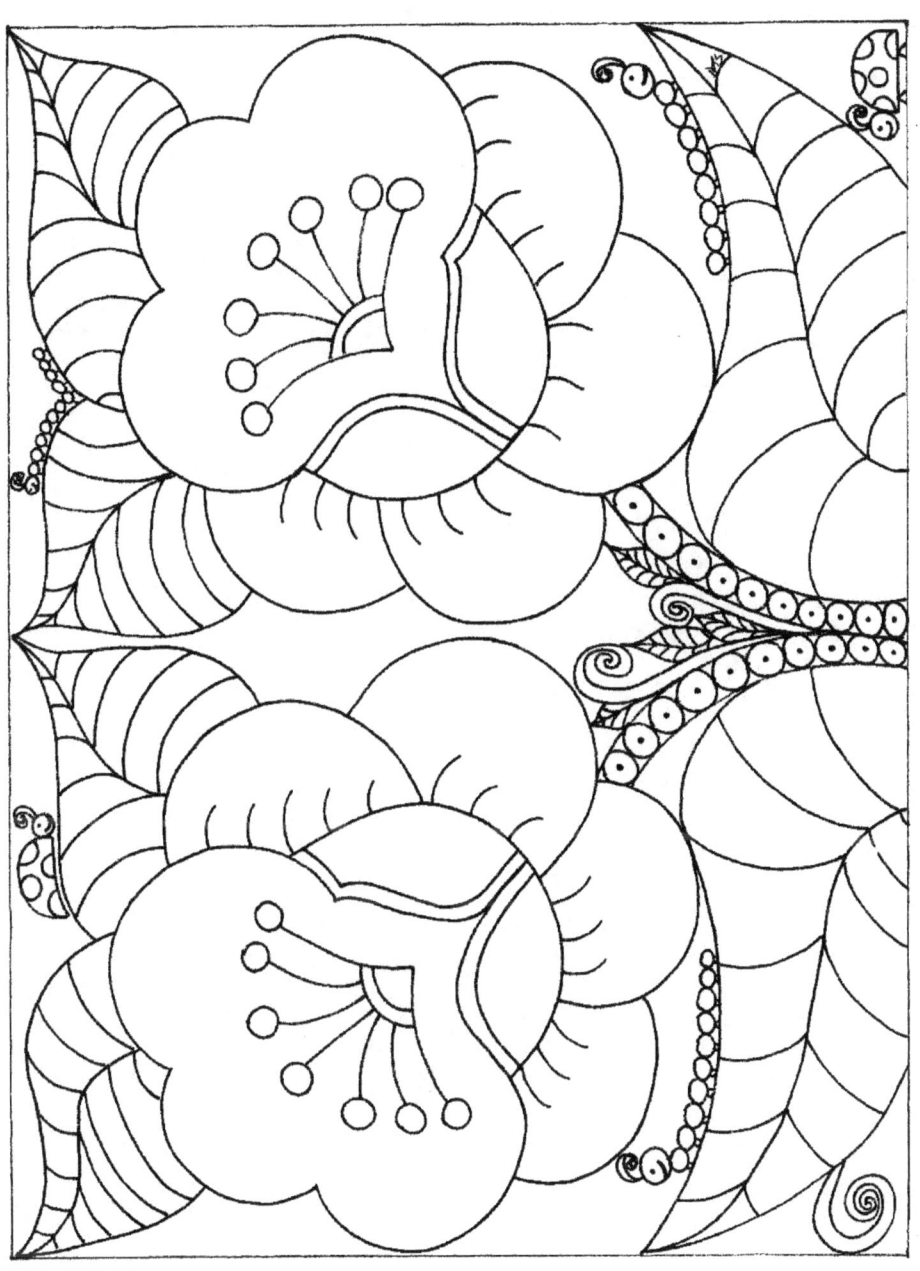

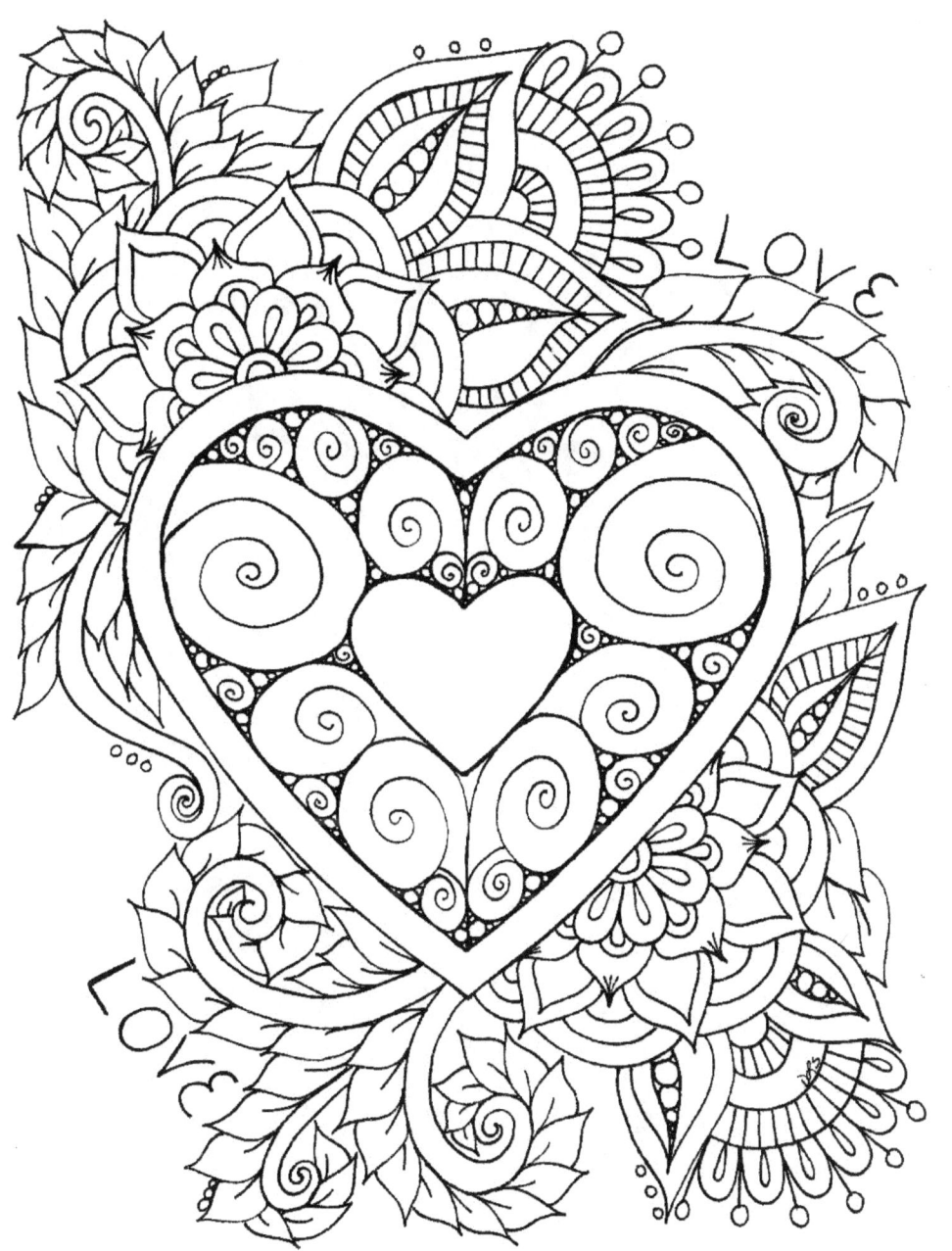

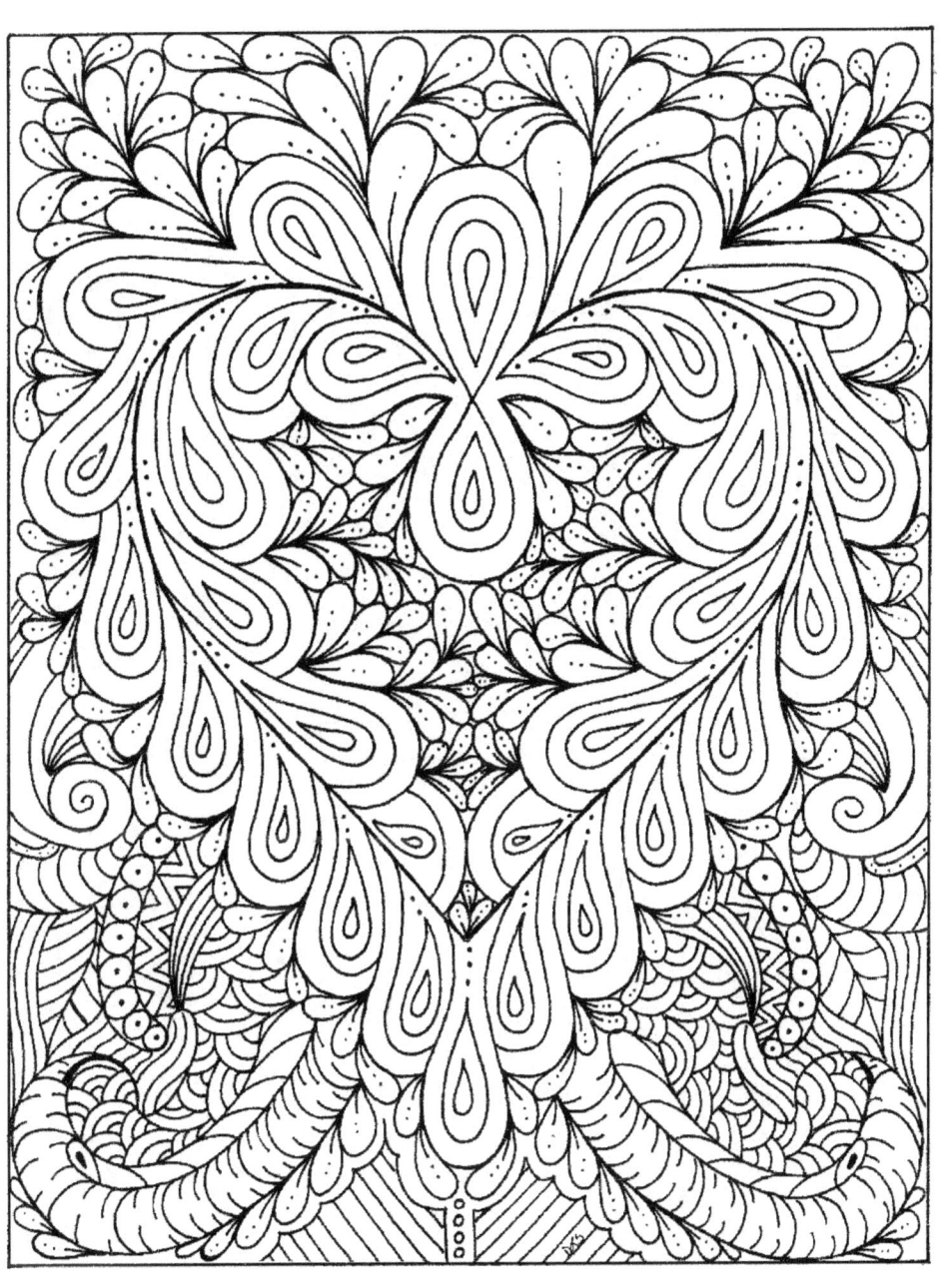

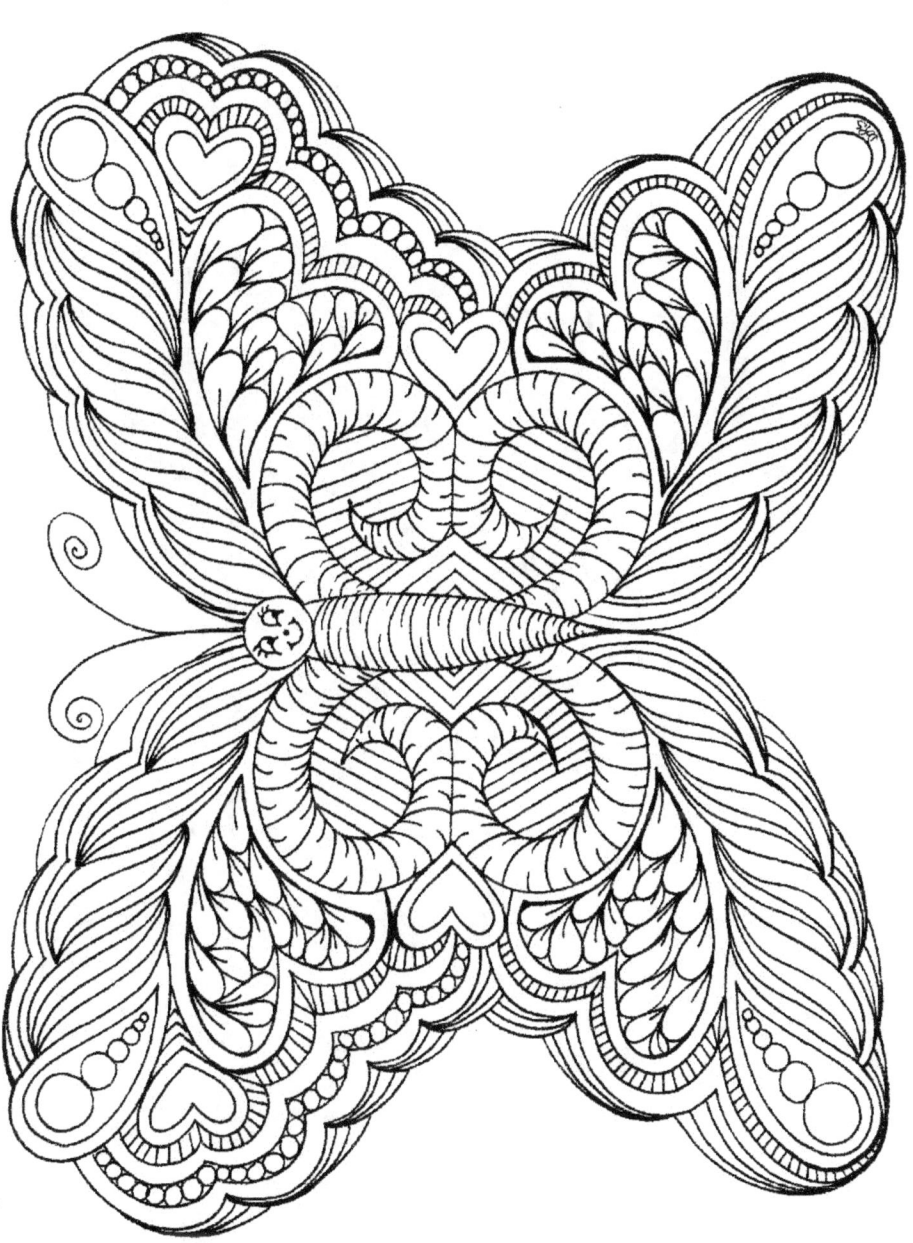

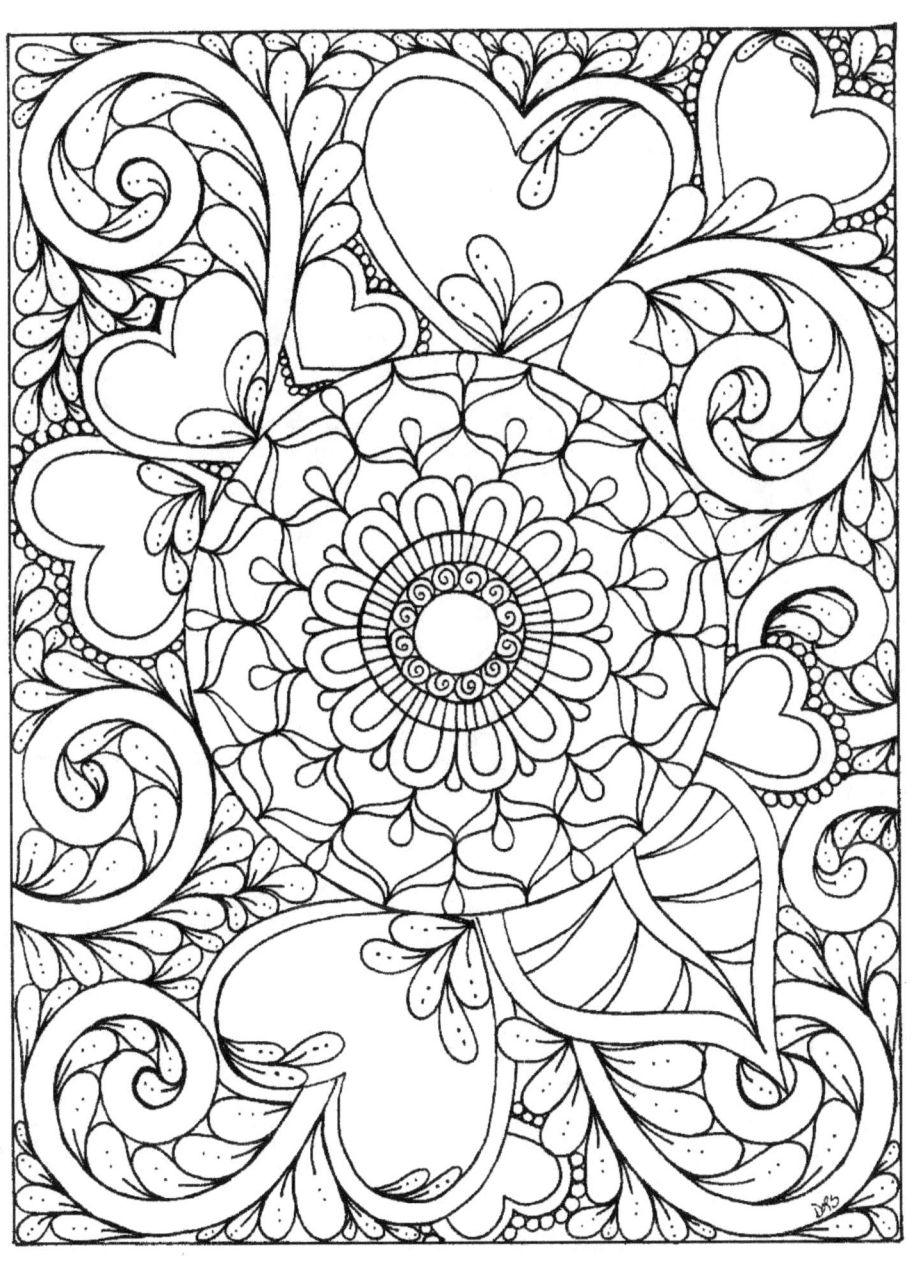

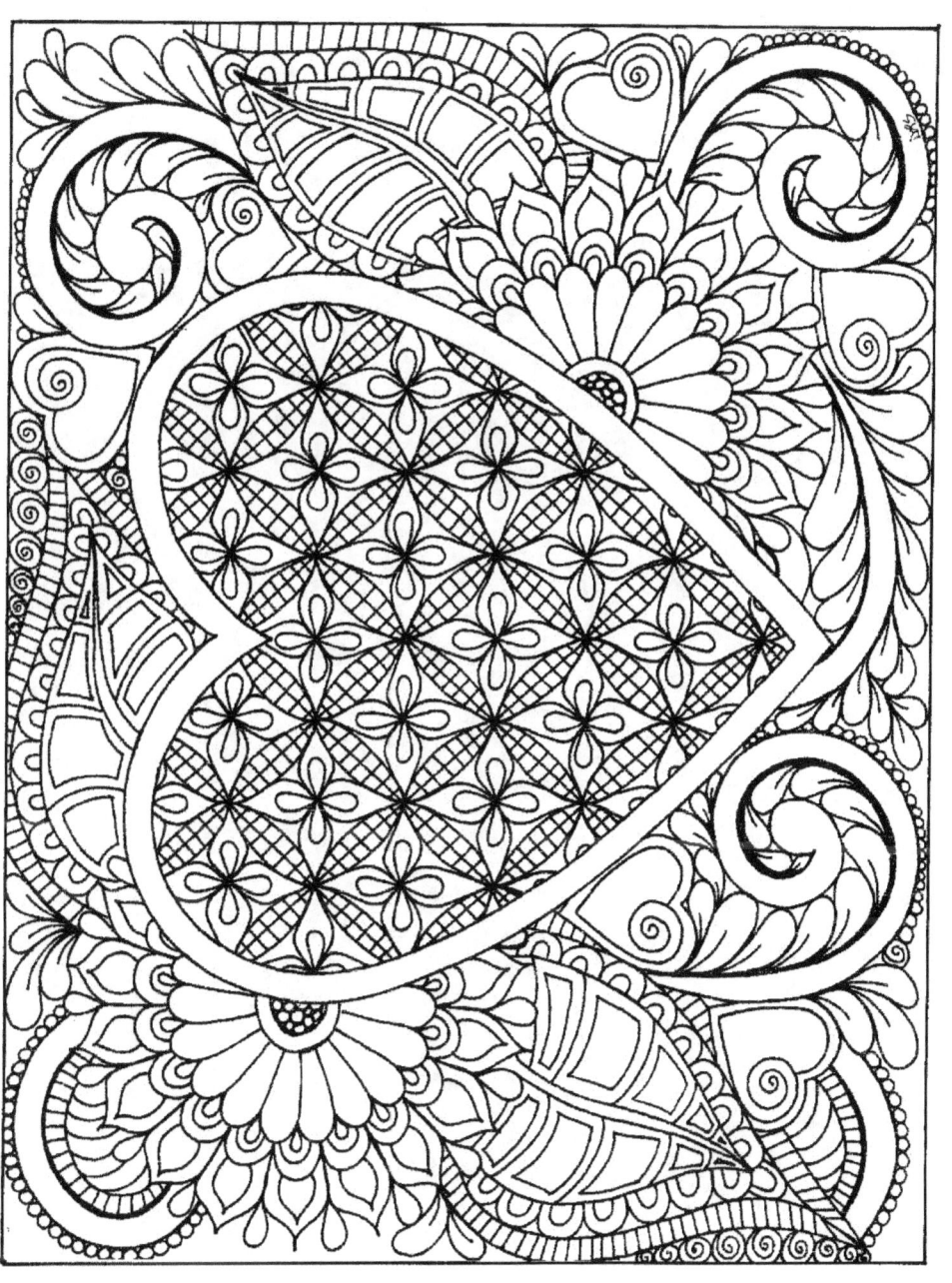

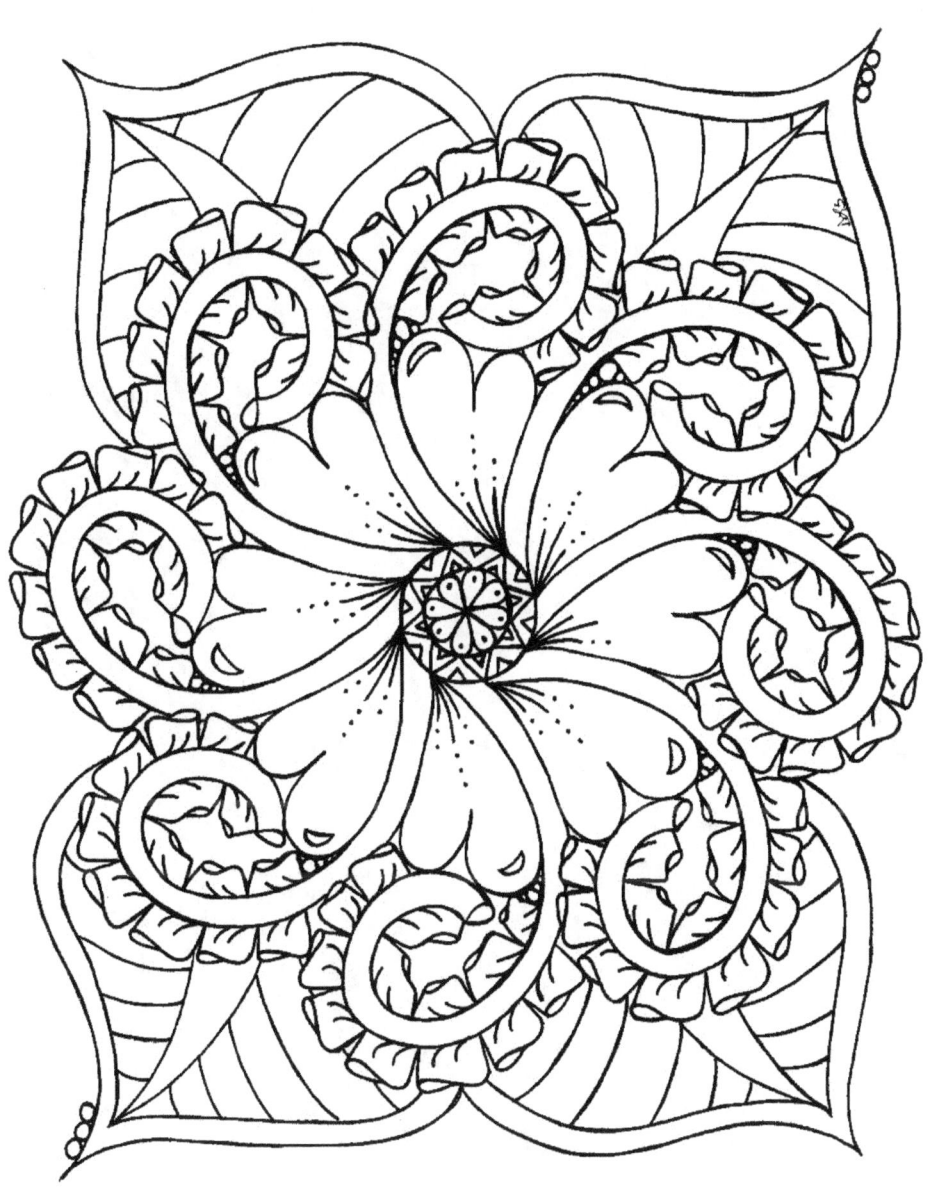

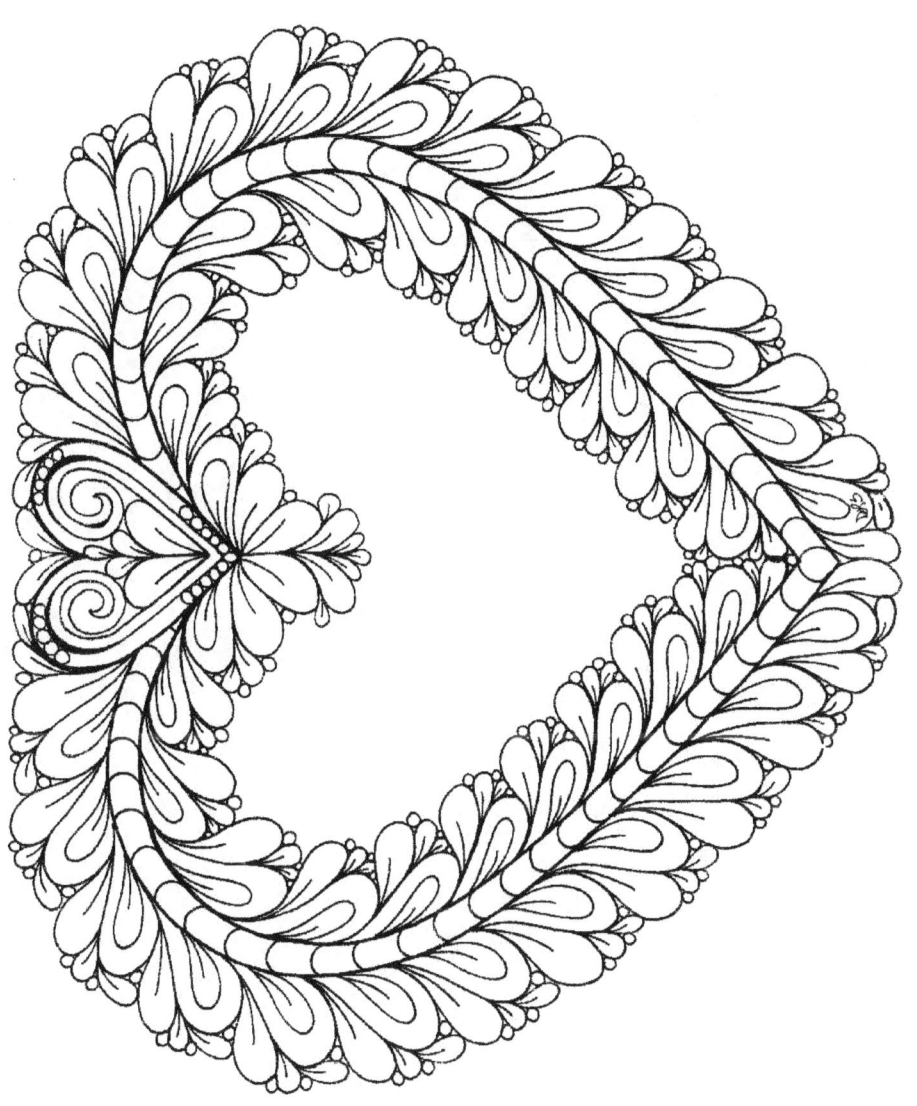

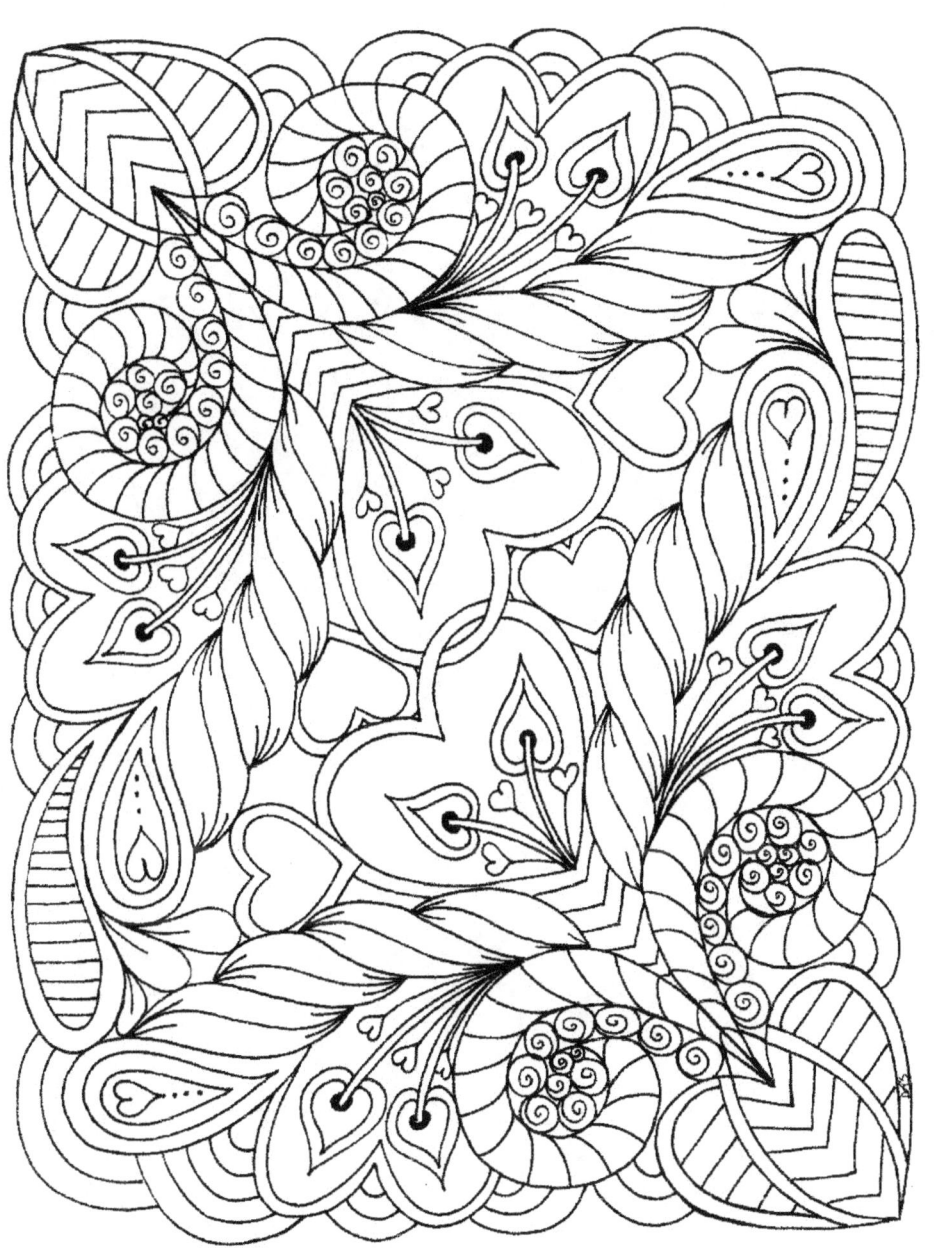

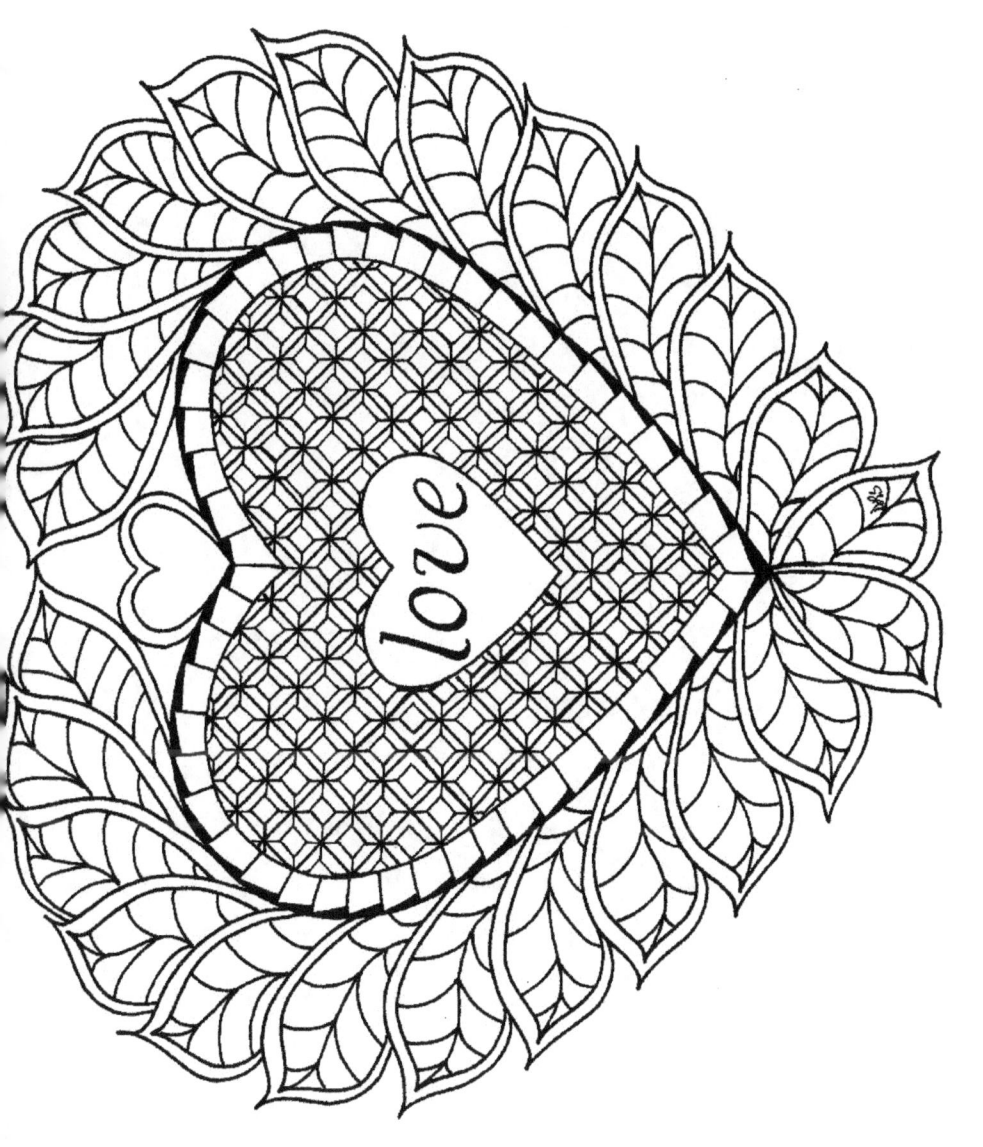

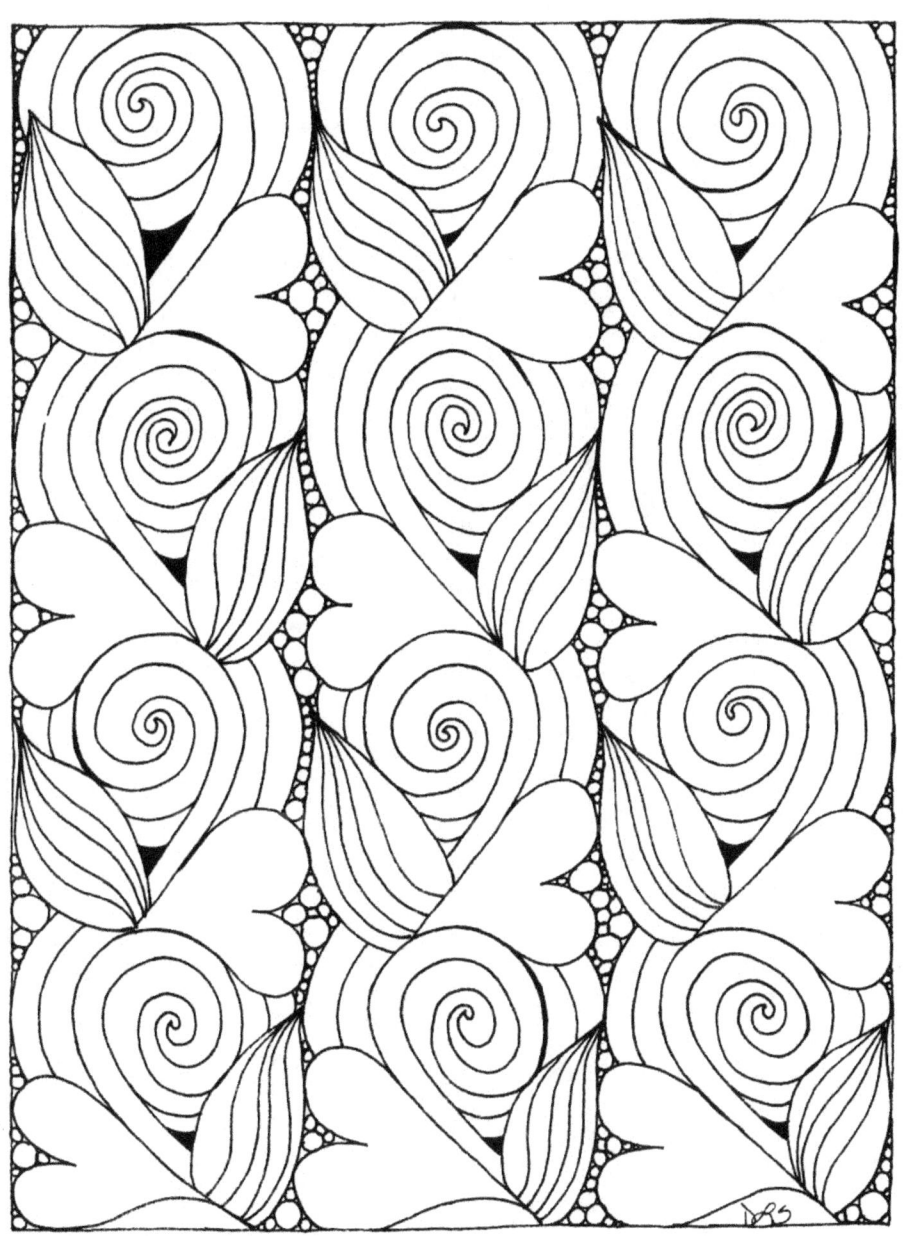

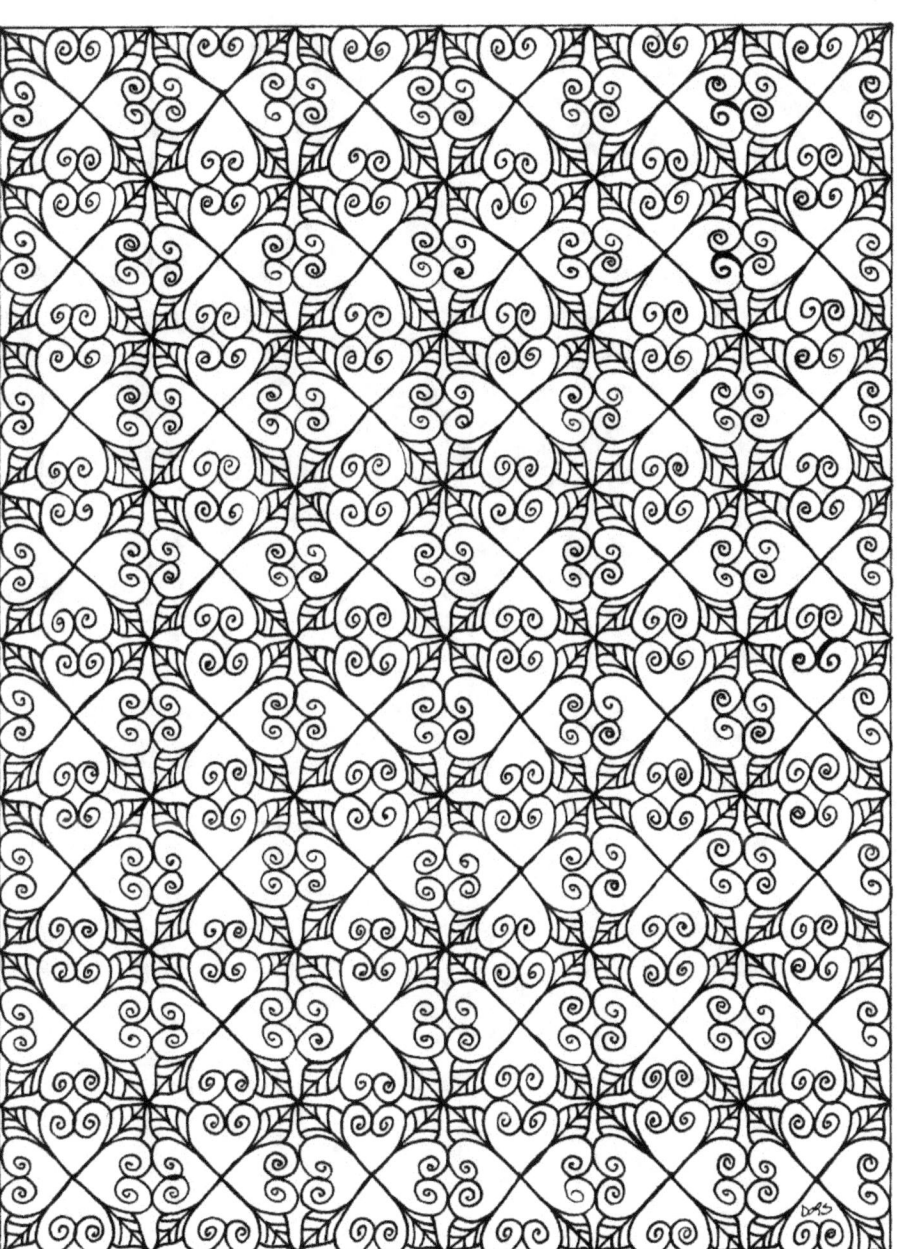

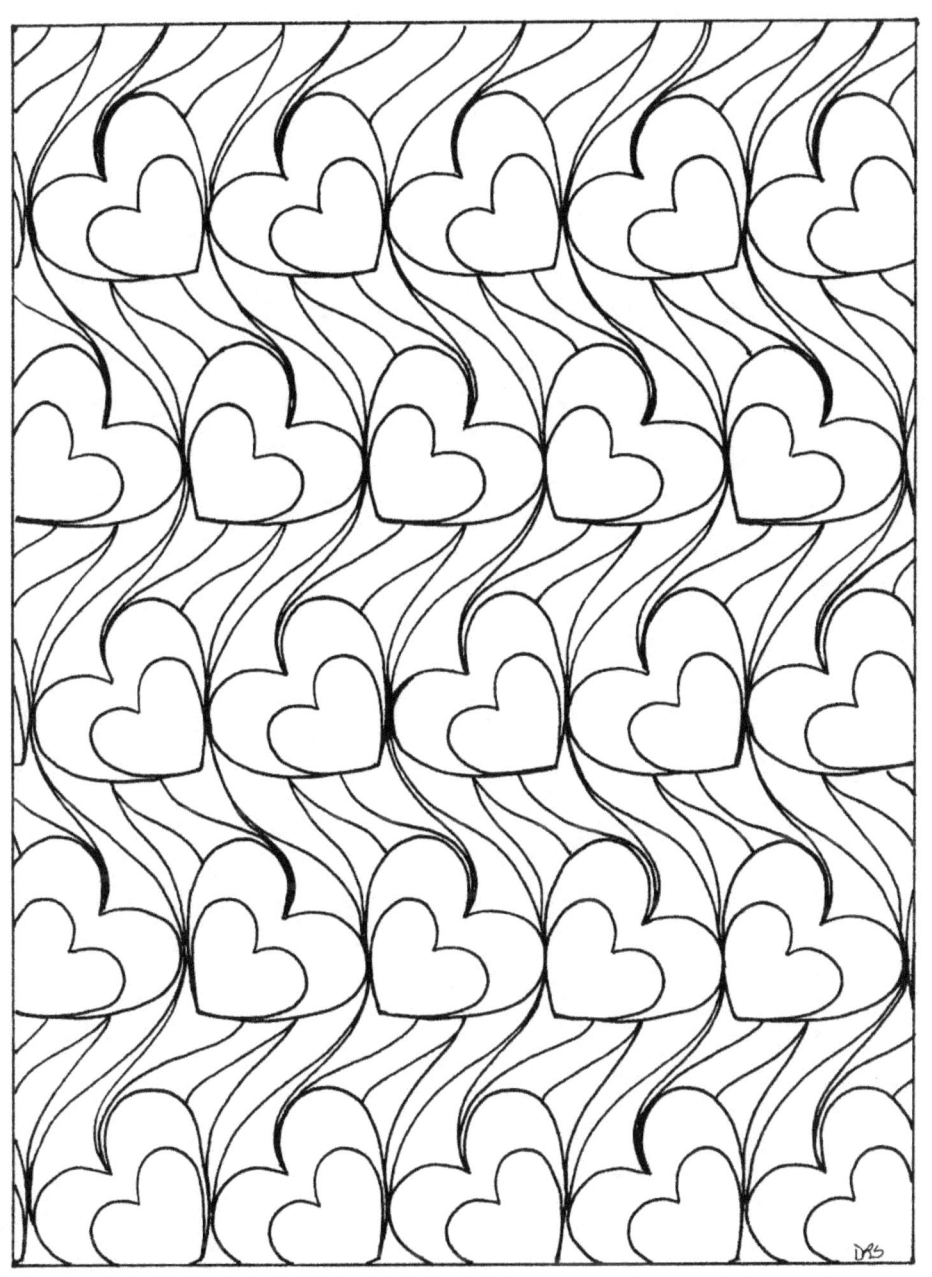

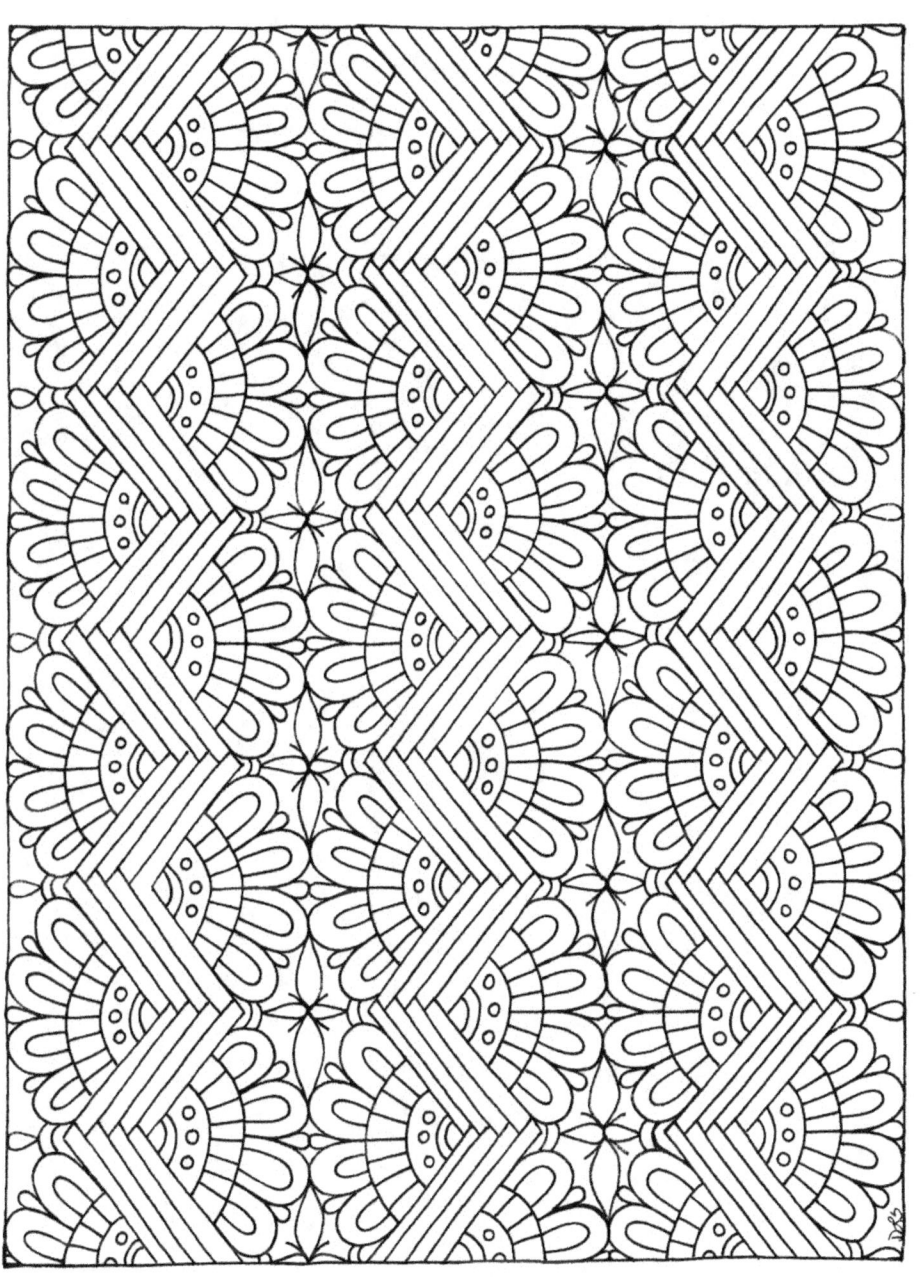

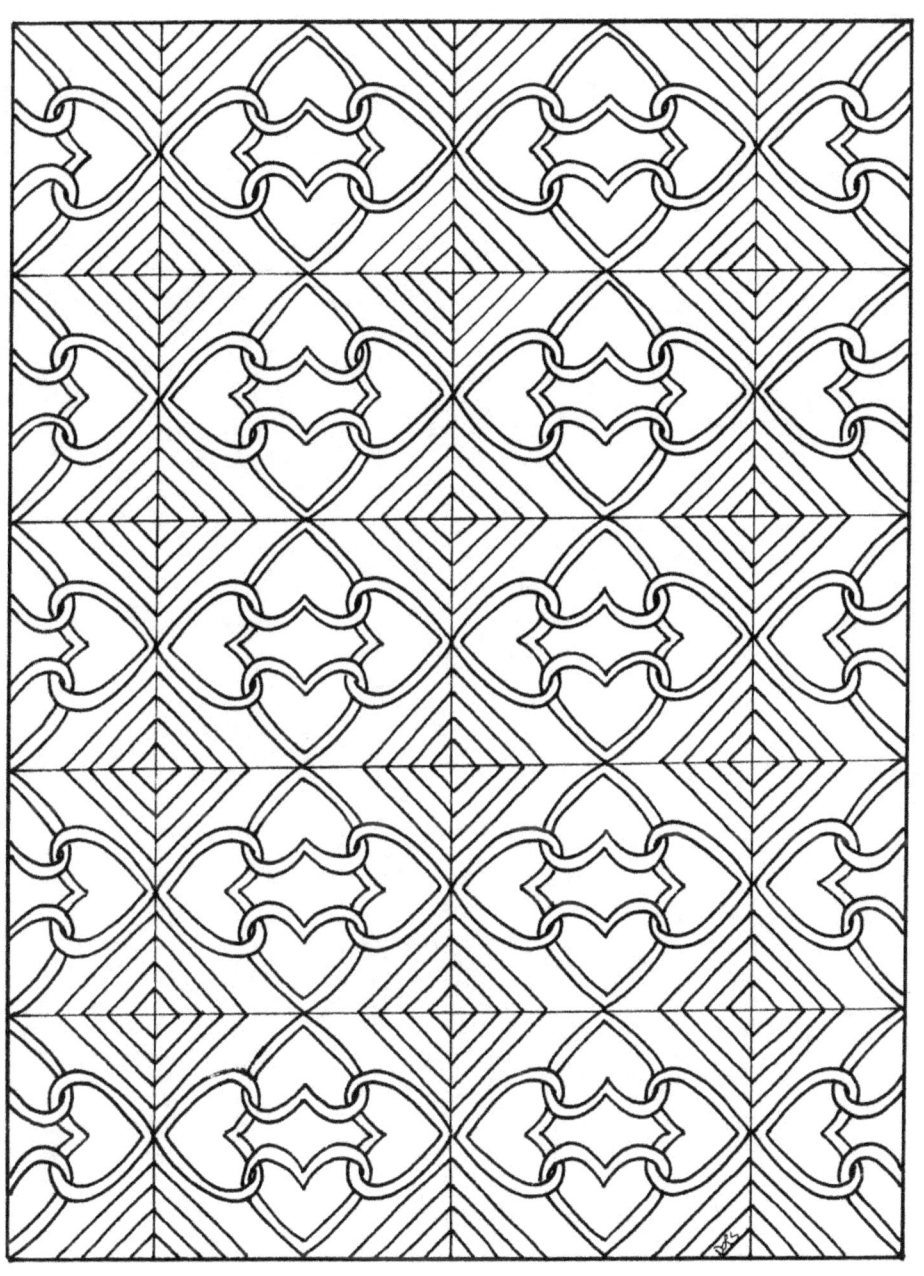

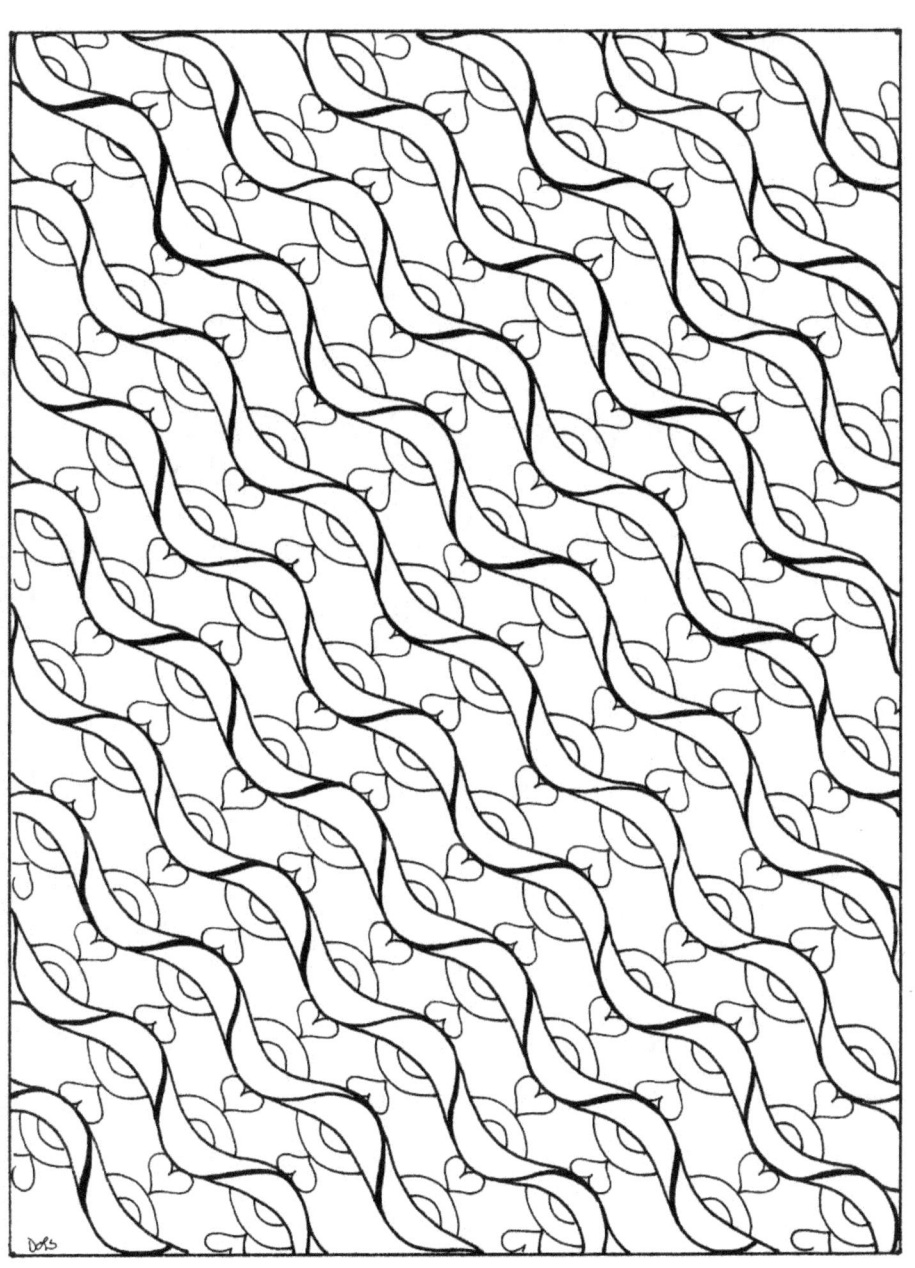

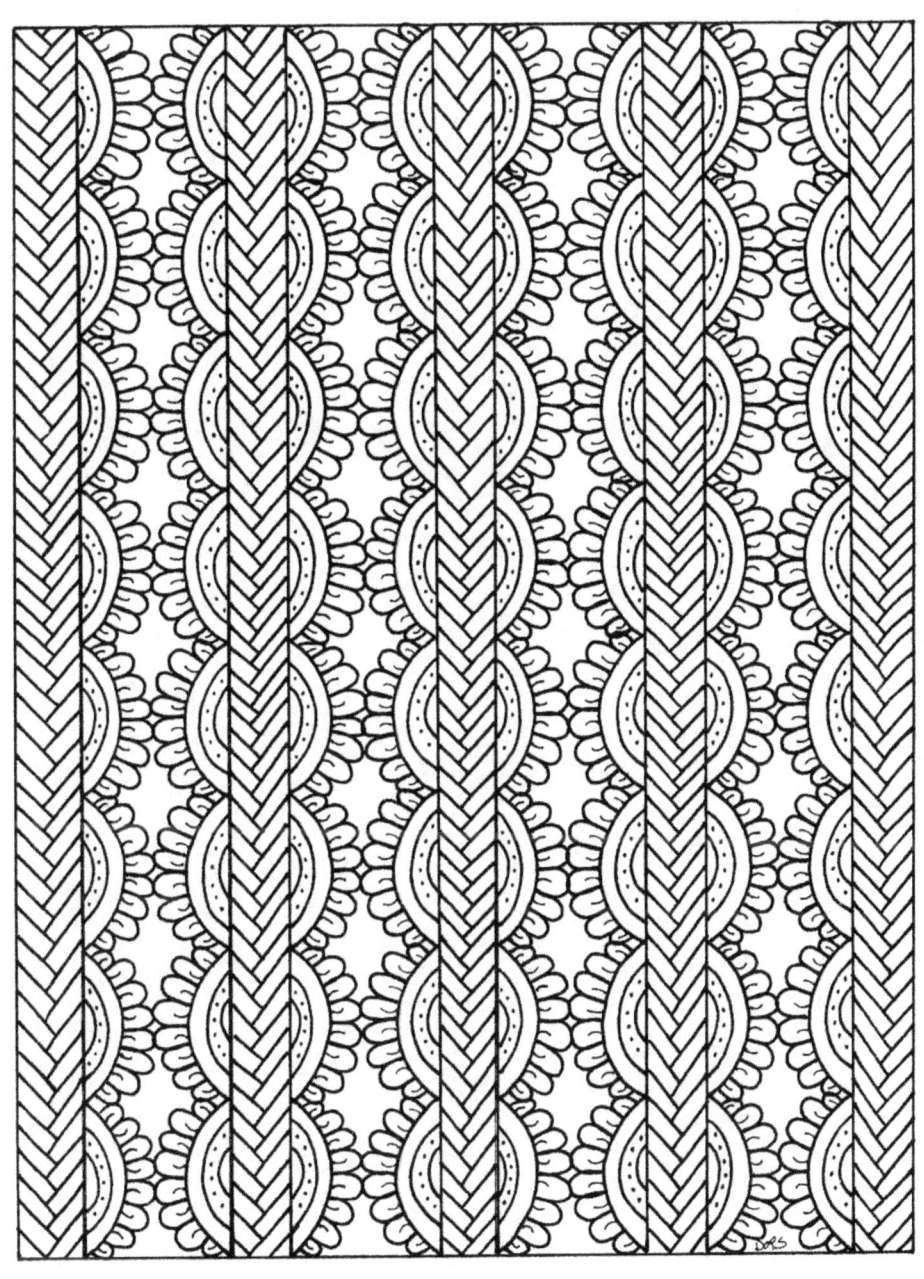

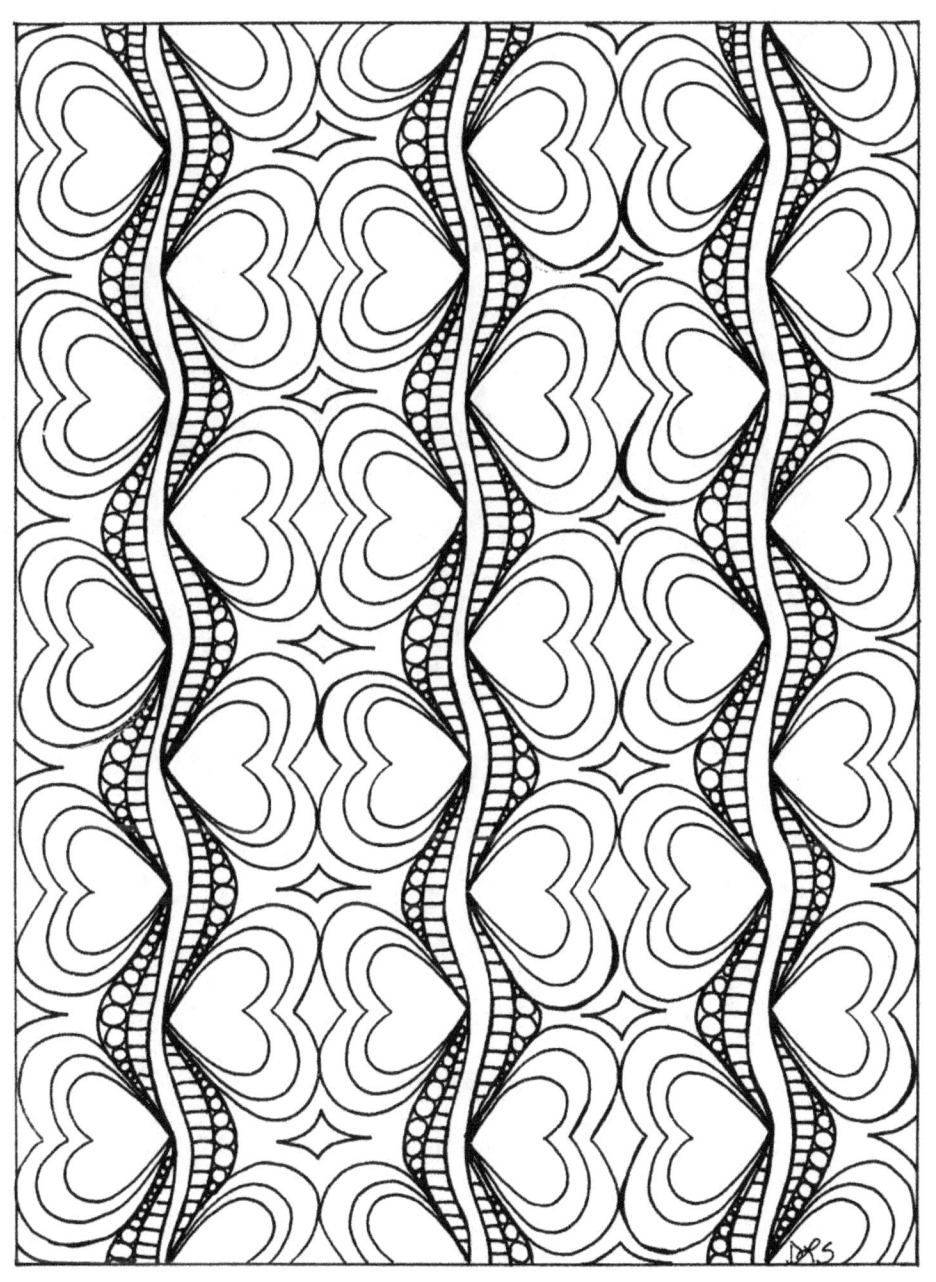

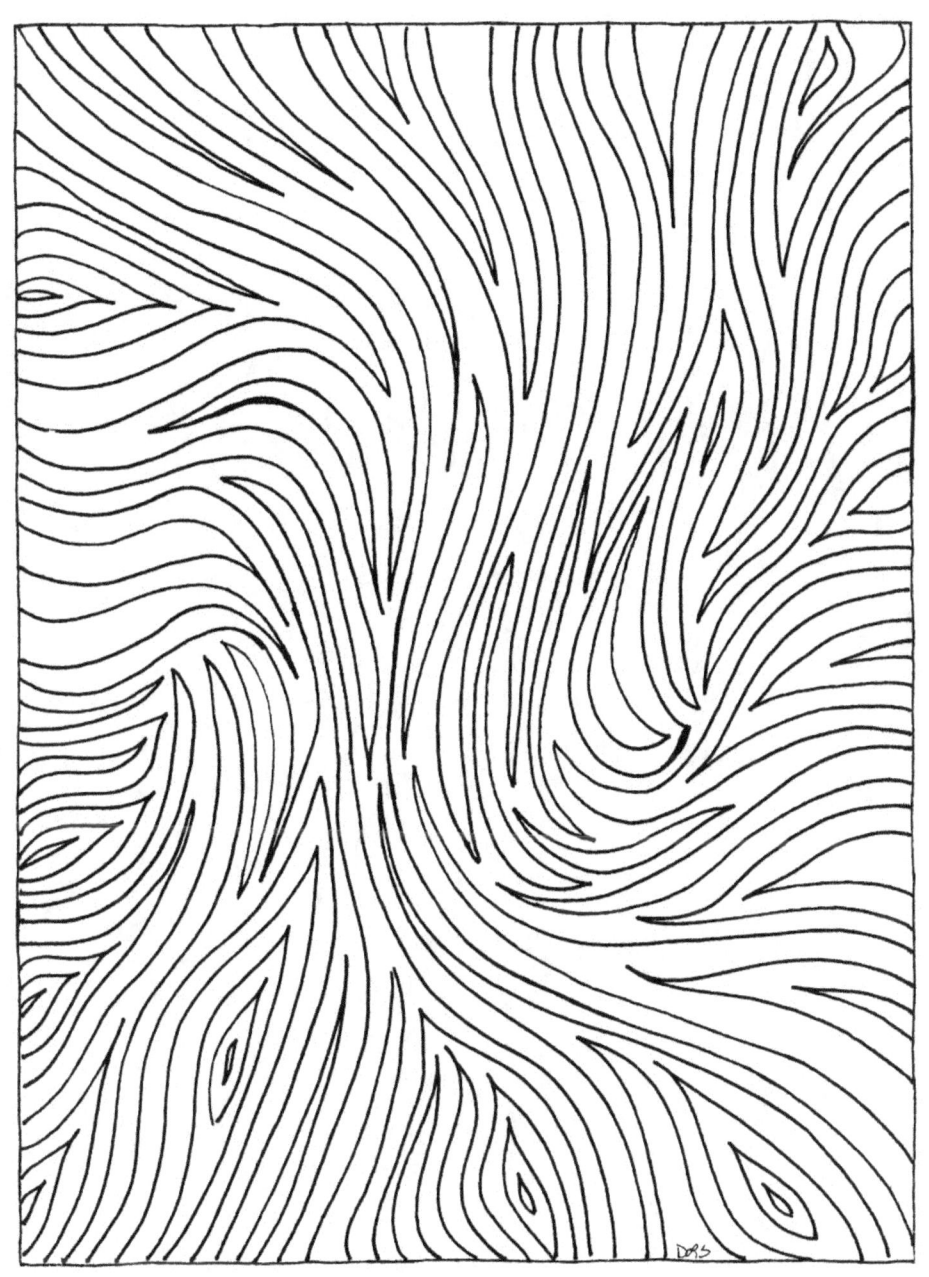

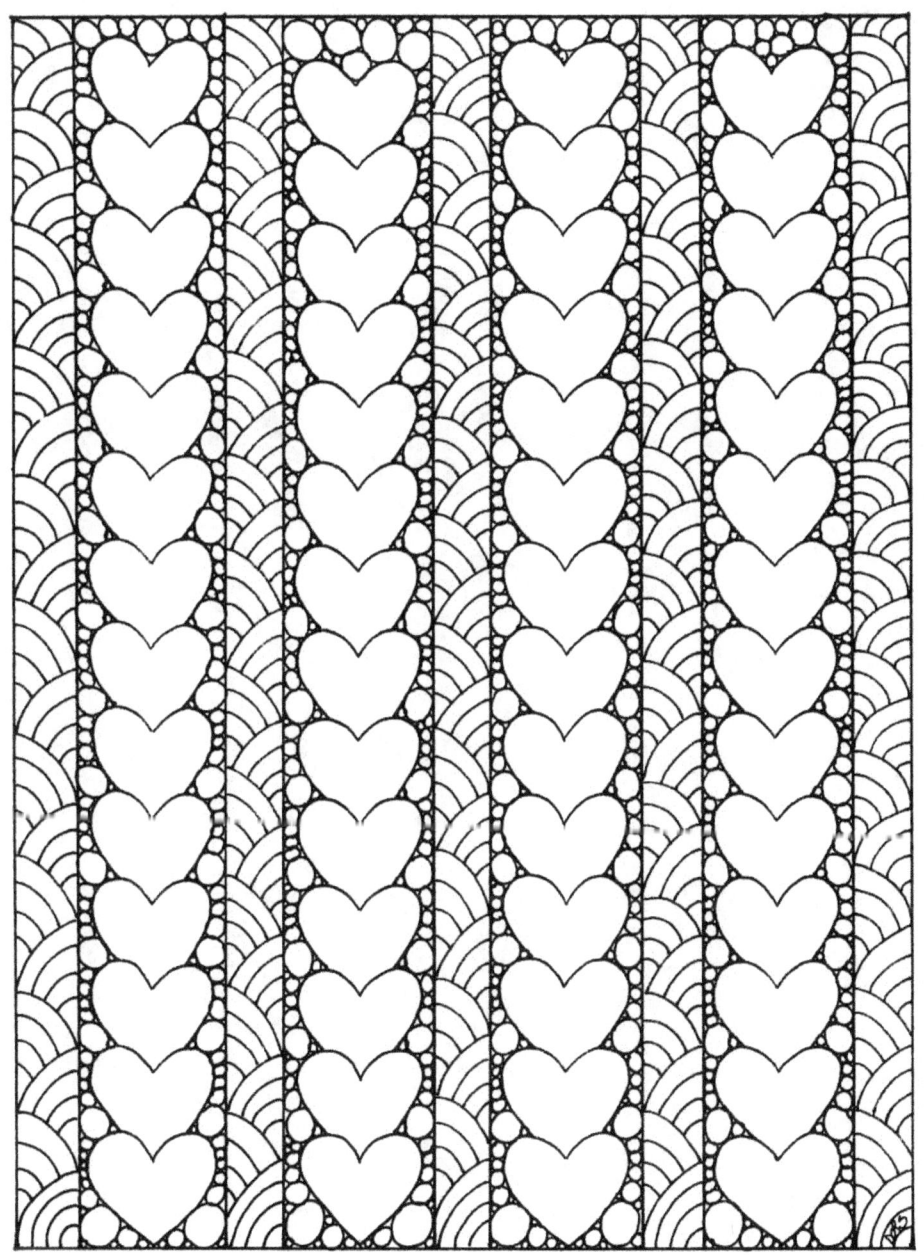

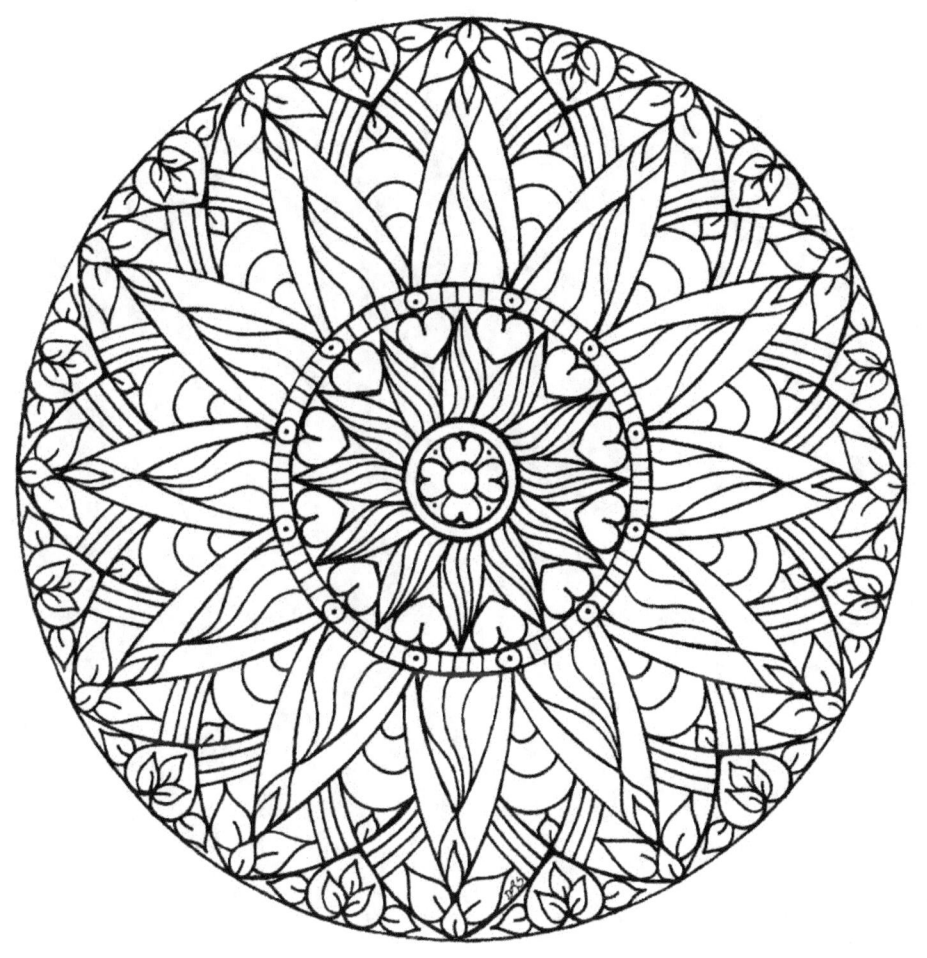

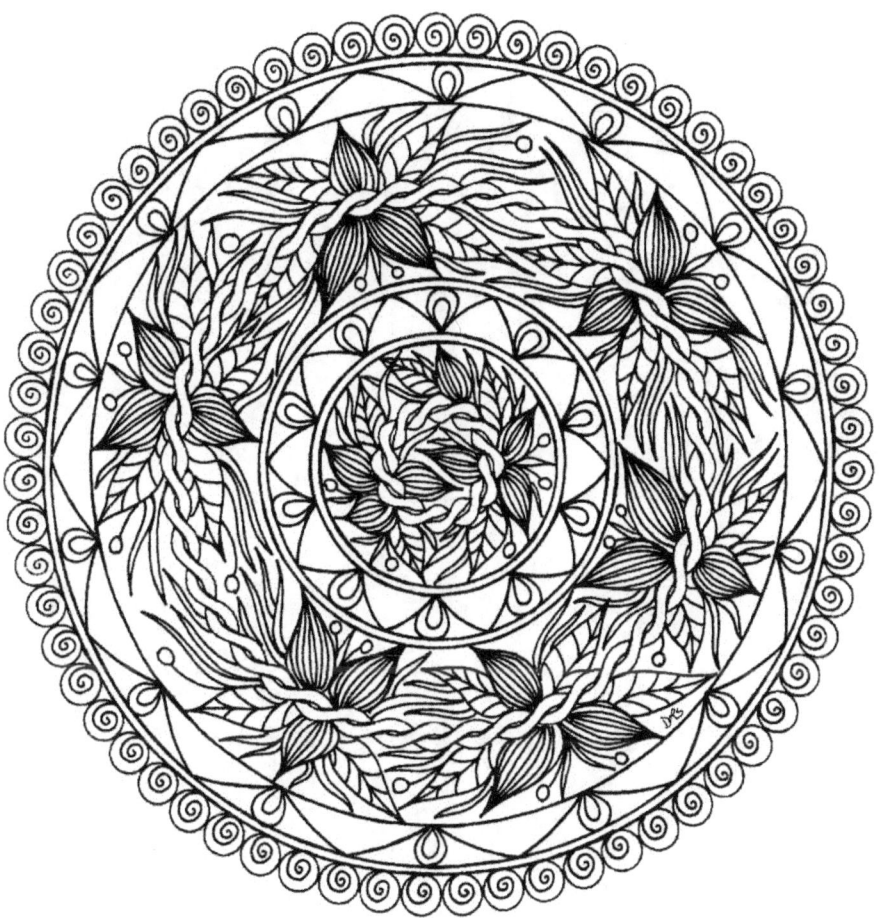

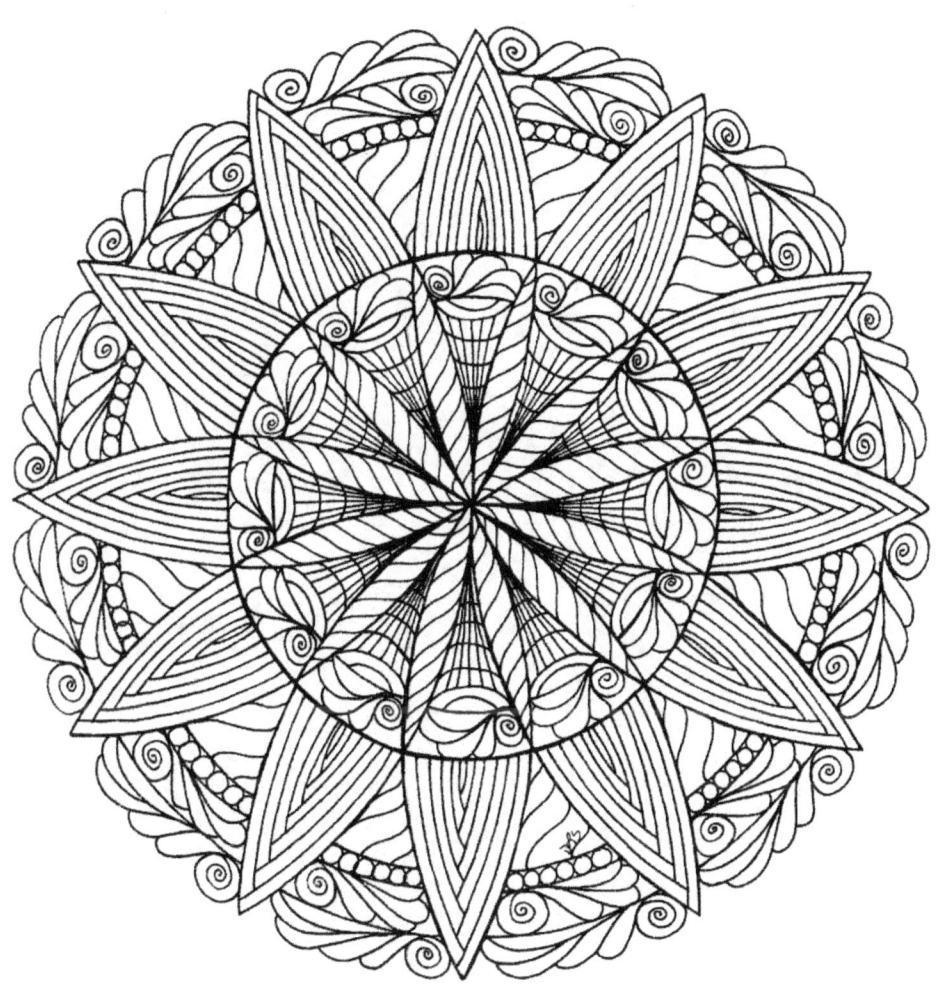

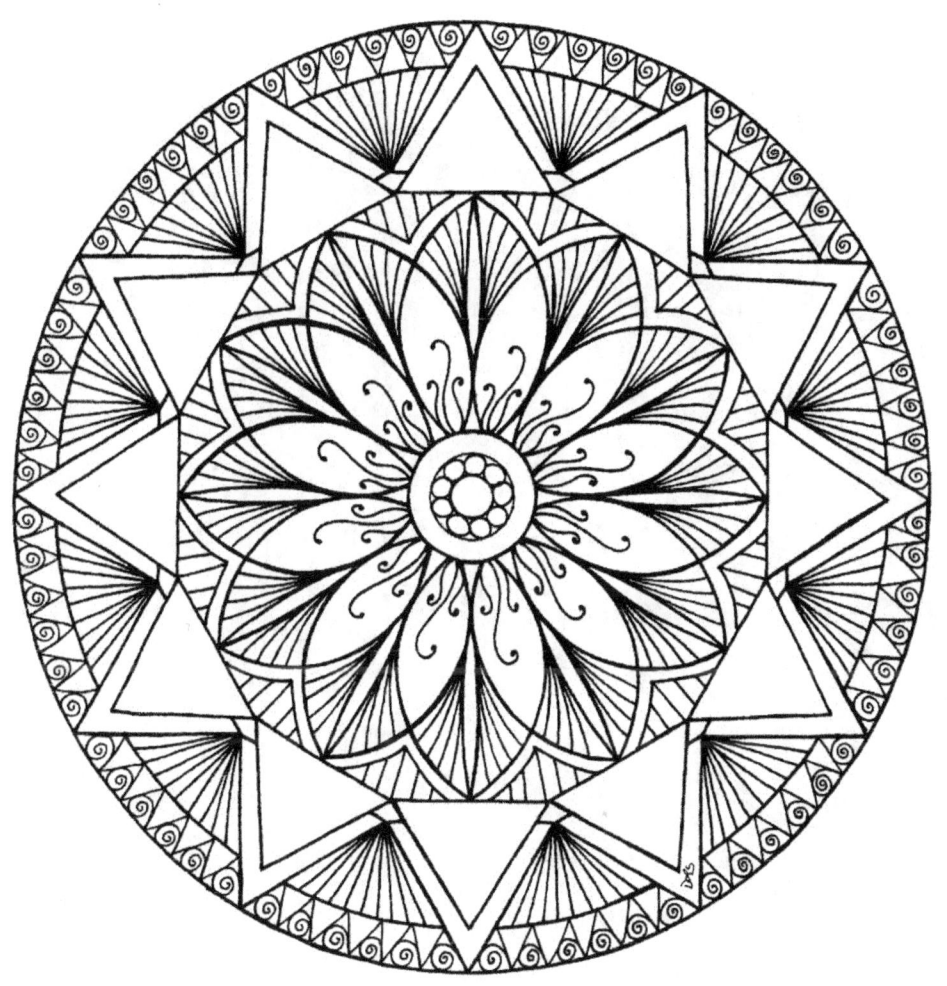

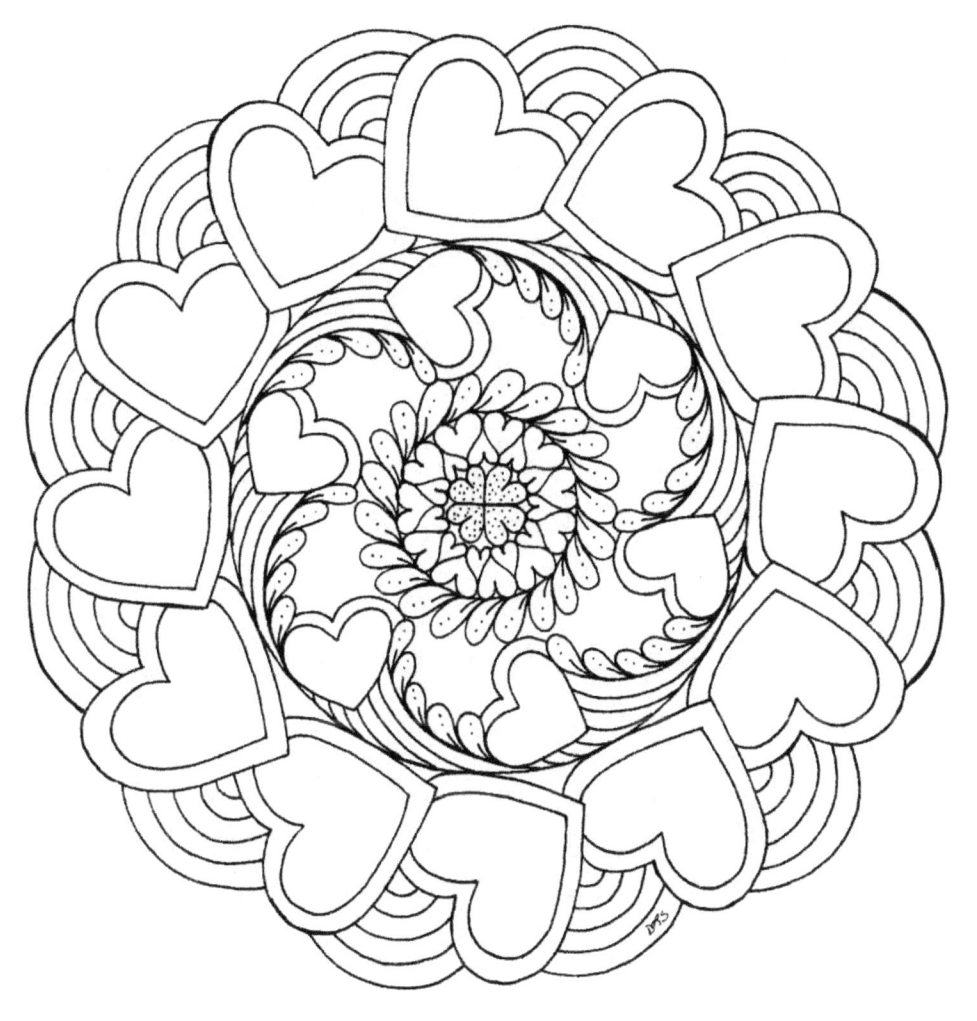

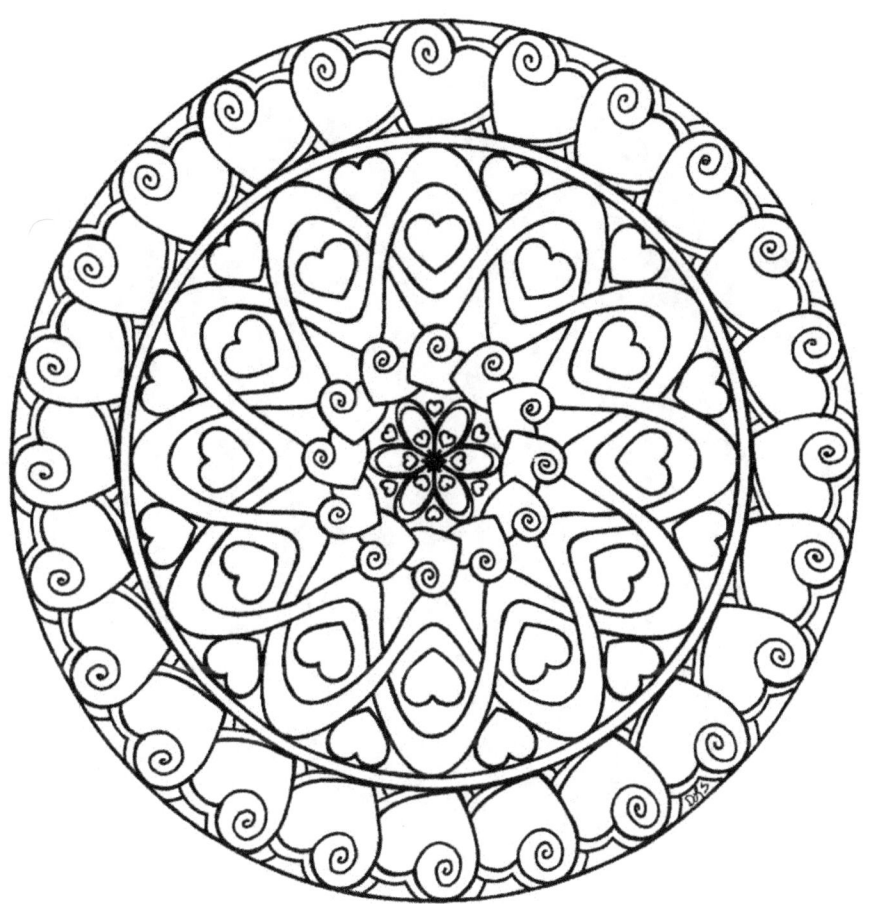

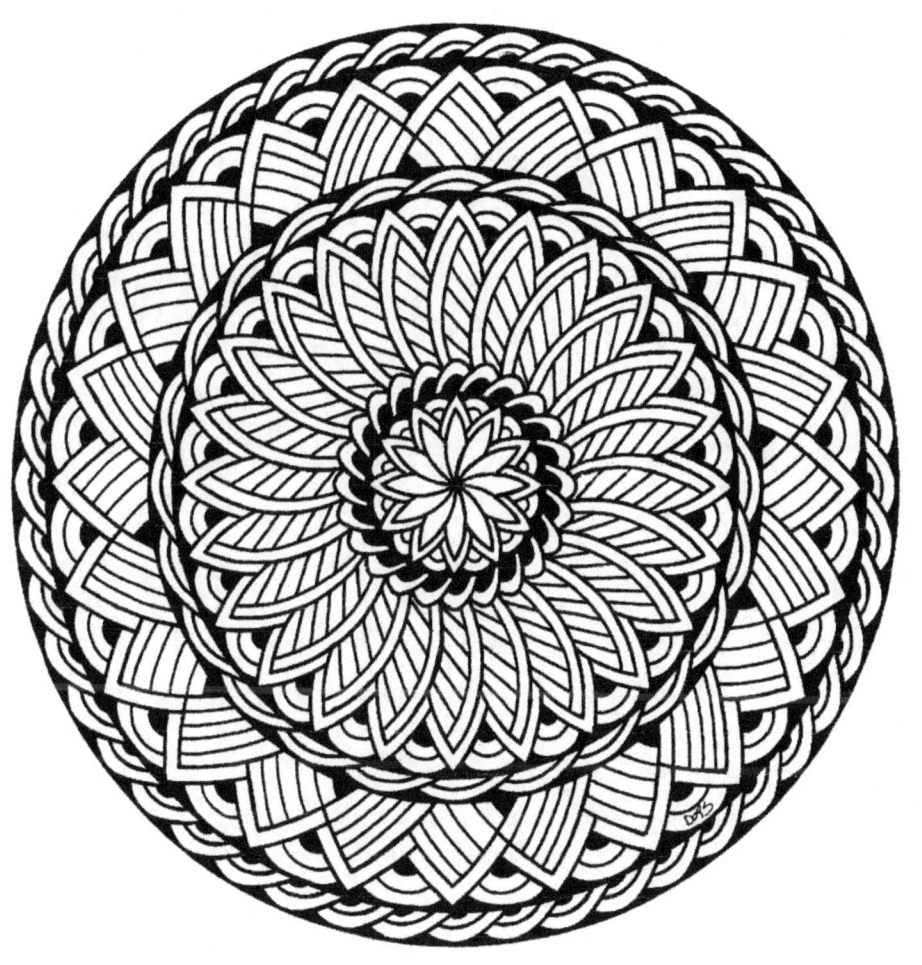

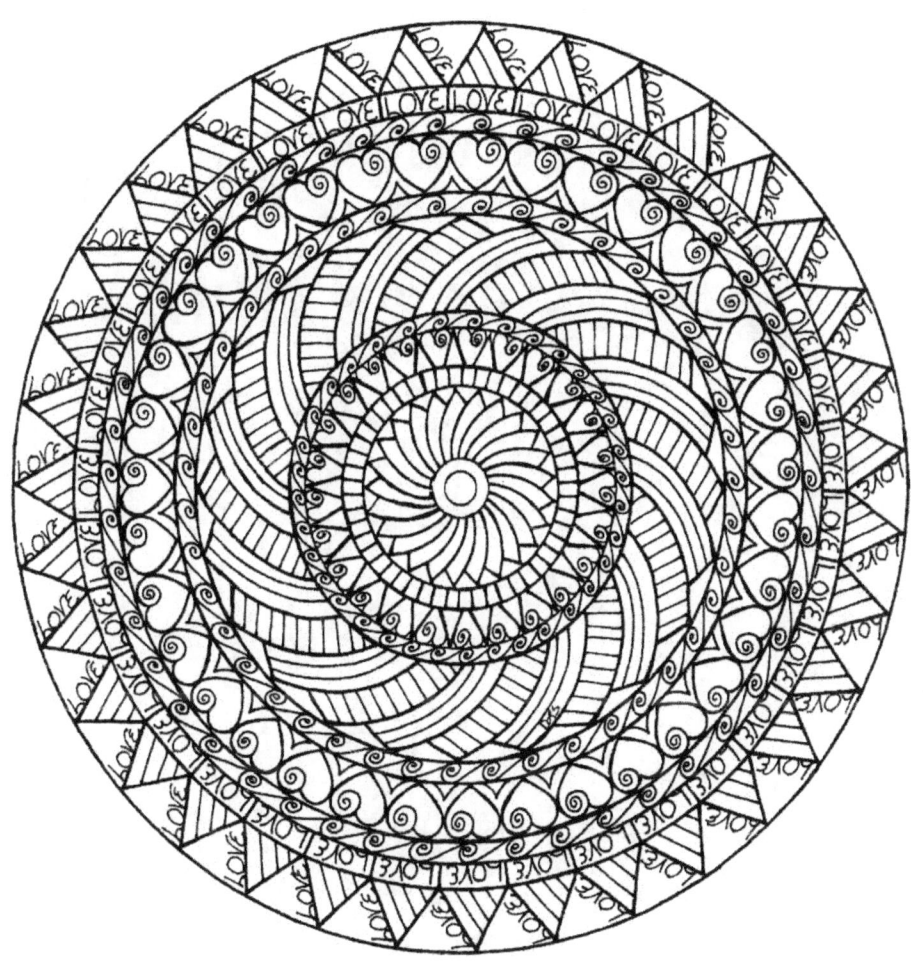

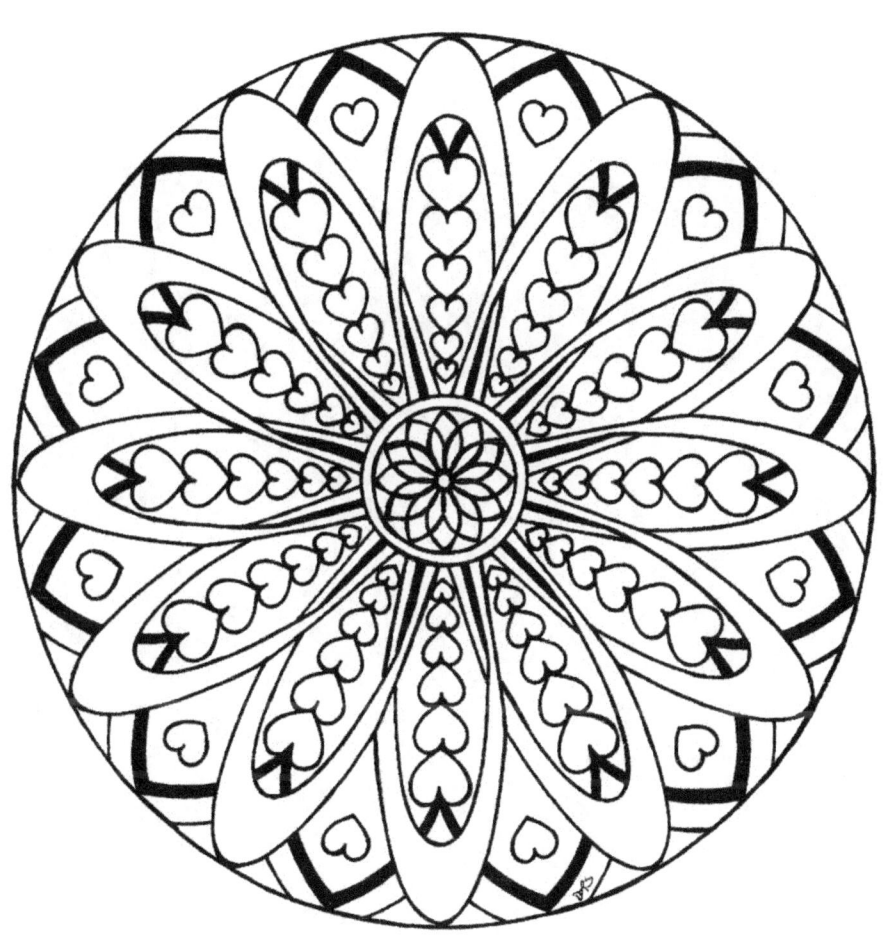

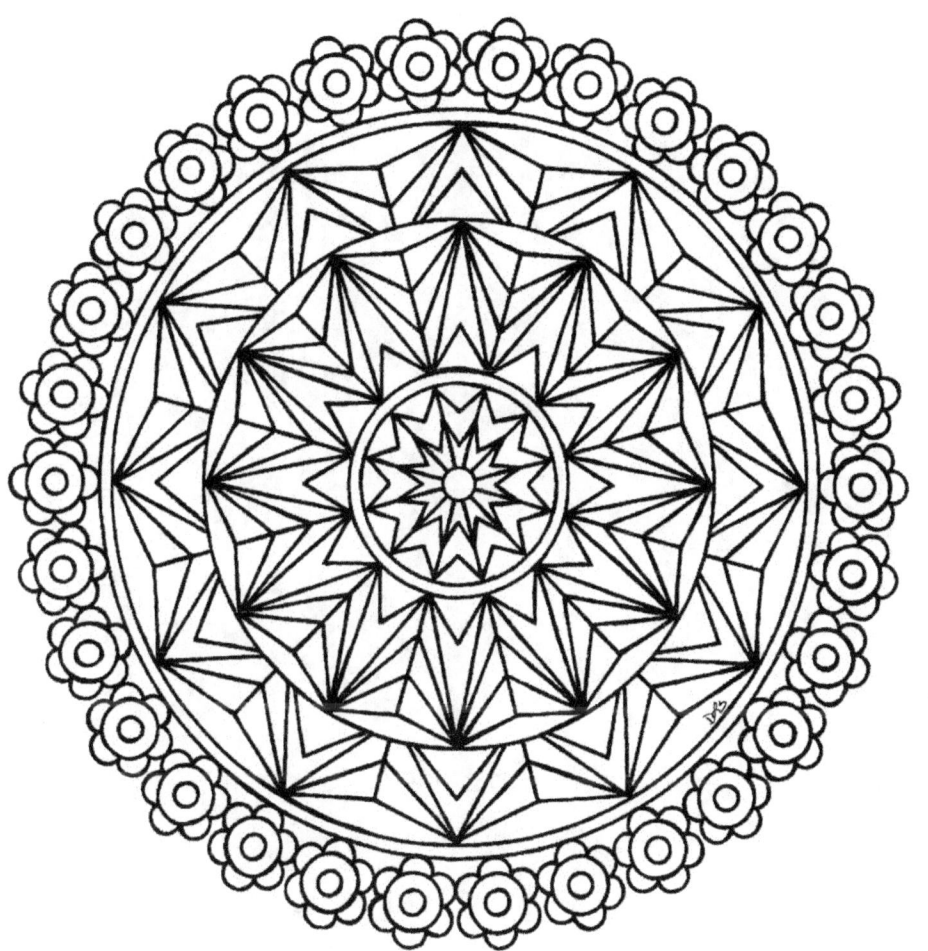

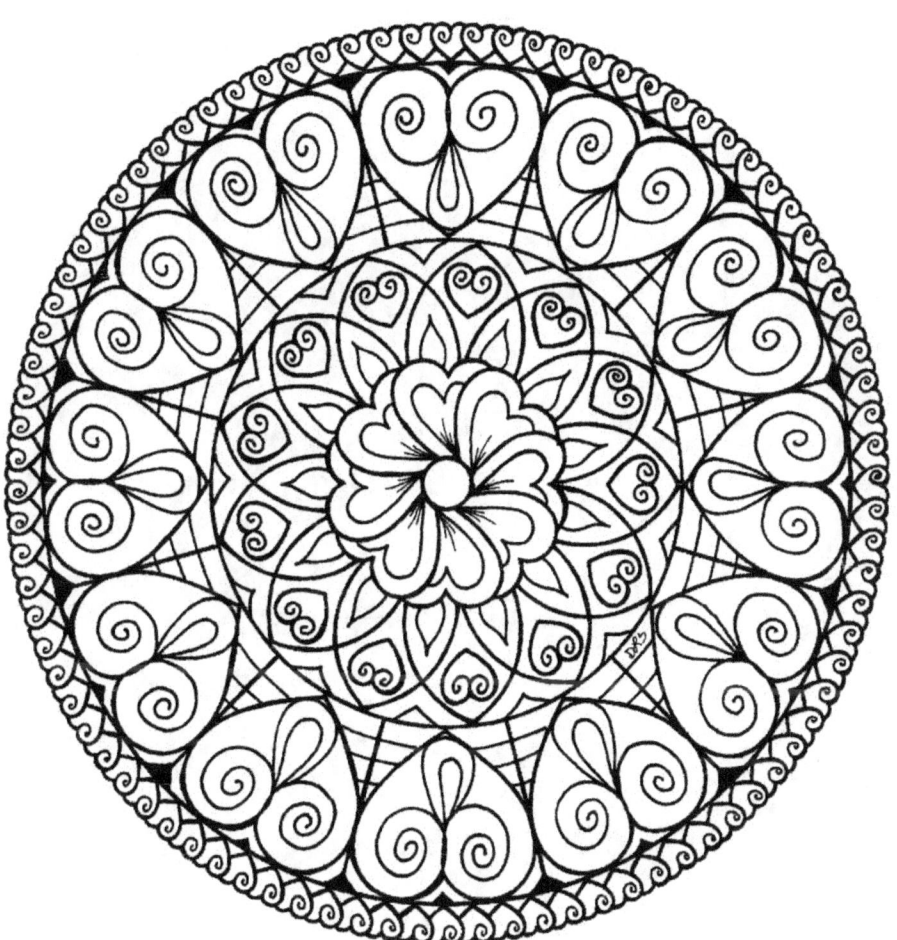

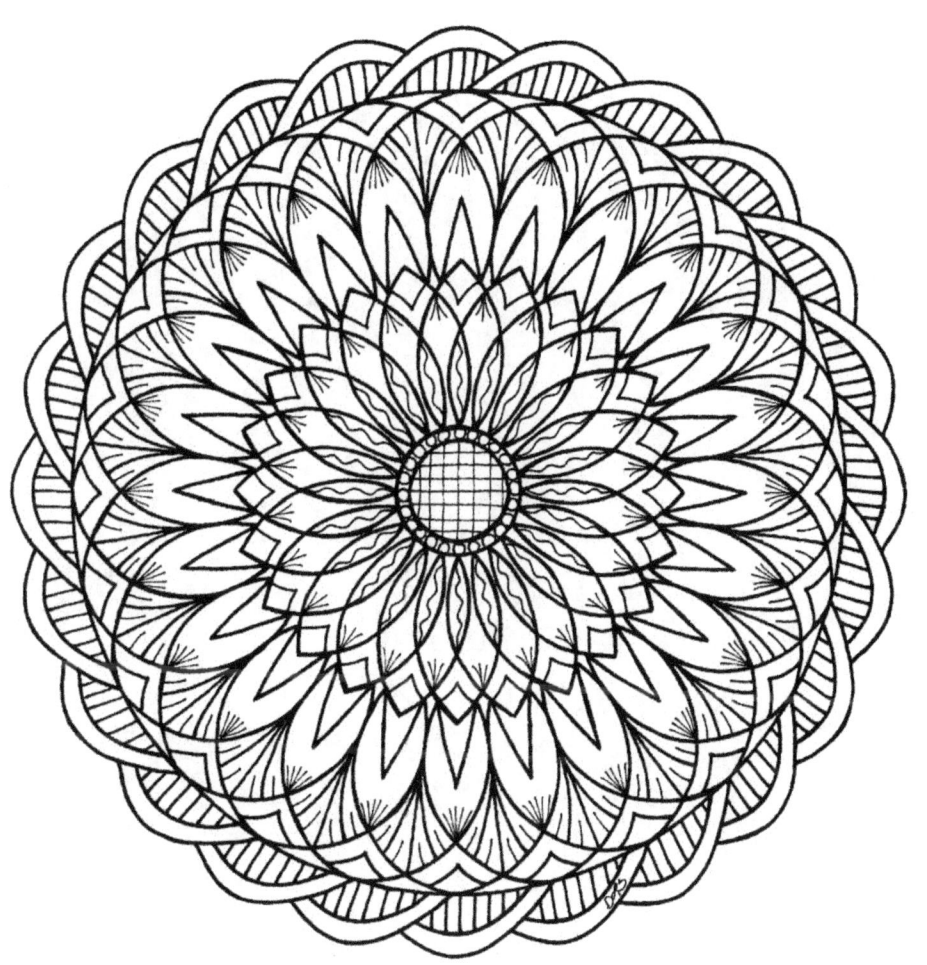

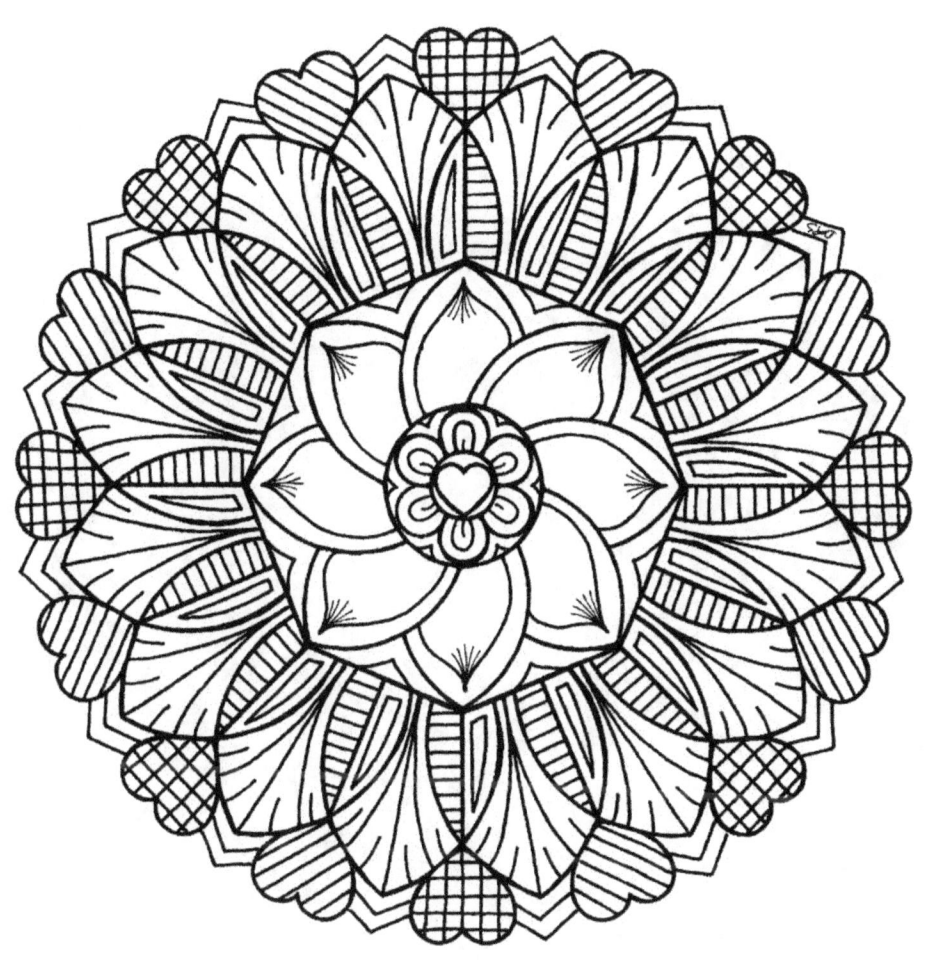

www.ingramcontent.com/pod-product-compliance
Lightning Source LLC
Chambersburg PA
CBHW060405190526
45169CB00002B/758